for Betty

The How
of Then

all the best!

Judy Davis

The How of Then

A Memoir

Judith March Davis

For my family with fondest affection
And in loving memory of Ethan Davis

CONTENTS

Acknowledgements   *viii*

Opening Words   *ix*

Book 1: "He Set the Standards..."

1   Revelation   1
2   Seeking Temple Court   7
3   Katy's Suggestion   12
4   No More Suffers   15
5   The Interpreter's Daughter   22

Book 2: Latchkey Kids

1   Whispering Years   29
2   Pentwater   36
3   Glen Ellyn   47
4   Poppy   52
5   Skylodge   60
6   If Only   67

Book 3: School Days Disrupted

1   Birdie and the Football Heroes   79
2   Dangling   88
3   Frank Sinatra and the Pants Pressers   93
4   The Jolson Story   98
5   Oberlin   103
6   Relapse   112

Book 4: The Farmer Takes a Wife

1   The Pentwater Yacht Club   123
2   Juniper Orchards   131
3   Claim to Fame   141
4   Great Expectations   150
5   Of Ironing Boards and Ovens   158

BOOK 5: CHERRYLAND NORTH

1	A Family Home	169
2	The Sixties	172
3	Easter Sunday 1969	177
4	The Record-Eagle	182
5	On a Darkling Beach	190
6	The Morning Glory	199
7	"This is the Editor Speaking!"	205
8	"Fine, Fine, Fine"	211
9	The Duke of Deception	215

BOOK 6: JERSEY YEARS

1	Do You Remember Me?	237
2	Honeymoon in Short Hills	242
3	How to Curtsy to a Queen	247
4	Learning to Hob Nob	255
5	Rutgers Newark	259

BOOK 7: WESTWARD HO

1	Retirement	267
2	An Earthshaking Wedding	273
3	The Queen Buff	280
4	The Million Dollar Photograph	284
5	Caring About AIDS	289
6	Birthing *Pagoda Dreamer*	292

BOOK 8: CANCER REDUX

1	Party B4 Parting	299
2	The Way It Went	303
3	Selling His Stamps	309
4	Military Honors	314

BOOK 9: HIS LEGACY

1	The Archives	323
2	Legacy	326

Acknowledgements

I am profoundly grateful to:

- Elaine Jordan, talented editor, writer, teacher and facilitator of a valuable Memoir Workshop.

- Fellow members of said Memoir Workshop for their critiques: Judith Crump, Kathleen Labb, Carol Rotta, Connie Thacker, Margaret Valenta and Bobbie Williams.

- Jennifer Longworth, format wizard and artistic designer.

- Family and friends who encouraged me to keep at the task.

Opening Words

Moth-like, memories beat their wings against the windows of my mind—seeking the light I hope to bring them. Most insistent are those transformative moments yearning to be shared.

May their illumination reveal key moments in your own experience and link us heart to heart.

馬

BOOK ONE

"He Set the Standards..."

"Memories are like tomb paintings... the colors still vivid no matter how many layers of mud and grime. Scrape at them and they come up all red and blazing."

– *Major Pettigrew's Last Stand* by Helen Simonson

1

Revelation

"FINALLY!" KATY SAID, both exasperated and exhausted, as she plopped into the last vacant seat on the tour bus.

"You'd think those women had never seen a cheap souvenir before," she muttered, "It was all I could do to keep them from dumping all their 'dollahs' into the open hands of those greedy vendors."

The bus idled as it waited for the dawdlers. As one of our guides that September 1993, the slim twenty-something woman had to count them off before we could drive back to Beijing. Later, I felt it had been meant-to-be that the only empty seat was next to mine.

No one in our tour group had opted out of a day at the Great Wall of China. We had all seen pictures of that ancient marvel stretching more than 2000 miles across the northern region of the country. But photographs could never convey the immensity of the structure that was begun in the fifth century BCE and completed in the sixteenth century CE.

Between the crenellated outer walls, the surface was wide enough for five mounted horses to gallop abreast, or ten infantry soldiers to march shoulder to shoulder. Seeing the undulating extent of this ancient marvel exceeded even my own high expectations.

Coming to China had been a lifelong dream of mine. My mother Dorothy Rowe was just an infant when her missionary parents took her there in 1898. Her childhood and early adulthood in that exotic land fostered in her an Asian philosophy that later profoundly influenced me as well.

What I knew best about my father Benjamin F. March Jr. was that my mother, nicknamed Doré, expected me to live up to the honor and privilege of being his daughter. I was born during the era when progressive parents wanted to be called by their first names. Because Ben died when I was not quite six years old, he became an almost mythical figure to me.

In preparation for our China tour, my husband Ethan Davis and I read "The Chronicles of Benjamin." In our early sixties, we were both retired, with time to devote to the detailed diaries my father kept when he traveled to China in 1924—at the age of 24. I had never opened them.

Reading these journals not only offered valuable insights about the country; they also gave us a deep respect for the prescient wisdom of the young scribe. Ben considered it important to record all his first impressions of that foreign land. He understood that ensuing months and years would cause him "to view the land and its peoples with the jaded eyes of familiarity."

Ethan marveled, "It's most uncommon for a man as young as Ben was to be so precise and detailed in his observations."

We knew that he later distinguished himself as an expert on Asian art before his death. And long before I finally went to China, my mother had also died. It was too late to tell her how moved I felt to be in the land she called home.

When I entered Beijing's Temple of Heaven, I remembered my father's account of how overwhelmed he felt the first time he beheld the brilliant colors of those intricately decorated ceiling rafters under the high conical roof. The feeling of connection to that young man who became my "Daddy Ben" brought me to tears.

The next afternoon, wearily returning to Beijing from The Great Wall, I basked in the glow of seeing those snaking stone heights that my parents had walked together.

Katy Ryor, the young art historian who sat beside me on the bus, was a Ph.D. candidate who held a Charles M. Freer Fellowship at the Smithsonian in Washington. She served as our designated expert and gallery guide throughout the arts-oriented Tour. Full of infectious enthusiasm for Asian architecture, painting and sculpture, the attractive slim brunette brought alive the context in which temples, scrolls and jade carvings had been created, and helped us understand the significance of each building or artifact. Sitting together for the first time gave me a chance to tell her how much I admired and appreciated her wisdom and her clear descriptions of the Chinese art and architecture we were se.

Earlier in the week, I'd mentioned to Katy that my mother and father had lived in Beijing for a few years in the 1920s. She knew I had been asking our Beijing city guides if they could help me find one or more of the houses my parents had lived in during that time. I had photographs taken by my father and addresses that I had gleaned from their homeowners' insurance policies. My father had also written the addresses in Chinese characters down the sides of each picture.

The guides had been ever so polite. "Oh, wurrah nice!" one had murmured over the pictures in heavily-accented English. Called quadrangle homes, such traditional Chinese residences feature four sides around a central courtyard. The design, with high outer walls, provided city dwellers serene privacy when their only gate to the common outside street was closed.

Our head guide explained, with a dismissive sniff, that those houses had been the homes of "the rich" in pre-Communist history. My parents were not wealthy, unless compared to peasants or rickshaw runners, but, as teachers, the two of them could afford to live in a home of modest size. One side held a large principal room with a broad fireplace and the only entrance. At each end of that room, a doorway led to smaller rooms. These were linked by inner corridors to the other sides of the square. One side contained bedrooms, another the kitchen and the fourth held servants' quarters. Today, several families crowd such a dwelling.

After cursory inspection of my photos and mumbled repetition of the addresses, the guide hastily handed them back to me and excused himself on pressing business. This scenario was repeated every day when I again asked how far such homes might be from our hotel and how I might be able to locate them. Brief, respectful attention, but no answers.

I gave up. We would be leaving Beijing the next morning, so I had to let go of the hope of ever seeing one of those homes. But I had become so accustomed to carrying around my small packet of photographs and other memorabilia, that it was resting on my lap as Katy Ryor and I rode side-by-side on the bus back to Beijing.

Suddenly, glancing over at the materials I held, the peppy young woman gasped, "What is THAT?"

"Oh, it's a copy of an art lecture that my father gave at Beijing University in 1927," I replied. "He came to China as a teacher of English and Latin, but he became so fascinated by the art of the country, that he devoted himself to intense study and was by then a respected authority."

"WAIT A MINUTE!" Katy exclaimed as she bent her curly head over my shoulder and read the name on that lecture cover. "You told us that your parents had lived in Beijing, but you never told me that your father was BENJAMIN MARCH!"

Astonished by her recognition of my father's name, nearly sixty years since his death, I stammered something about not having dreamed that his identity would have any meaning to her.

"OH, but of *course* I know of Benjamin March," Katy enthused. "He was a very important interpreter of Asian art for Western scholars. I've read all of his books and I drew heavily upon his work in my own research."

"But, so much scholarship has gone on since he died," I stammered, astonished. "I had no idea that anyone studying today would still know of his work."

"Yes, of course he wrote and taught many years ago and many other books have been published since then," Katy said. "But he's still read because he set the standards for the critical examination of Chinese painting."

Inhaling sharply, I tried to take in those thrilling words. I had never imagined that anyone still knew my father's name, much less that they continued to learn from the work he had done.

As I gazed out the windows of the bus, the steep hills and lacy pine trees of northern China passed in a blur before my damp eyes. Until that moment, I had thought of my father's life as history. I had believed my mother's account of his career, of course, and I had read letters that men of consequence had written to her following his early death. Even as they expressed sympathy at her grievous loss, they emphasized how keenly he would be missed in the field of Asian Art. When he died, Ben was curator of Oriental Art at the Detroit Institute of the Arts and a lecturer at the University of Michigan.

I knew that despite his youth he was a leading figure in his profession. But that was so many years ago. It was profoundly heartwarming to learn how long my father's legacy had endured. I wish my mother could know.

As the bus rumbled back to Beijing, I wished again that I could see the courtyard home where my parents had lived in 1926.

2

Seeking Temple Court

THE MINUTE the tour bus pulled up to our lavish western-style hotel in Beijing, Katy Ryor scrambled off and dashed away. I didn't even wonder what she might be up to. Her work had nothing to do with me.

Soon, I saw our young art historian huddled with the leading local city guide, gesturing expansively while speaking in rapid, earnest Chinese. She was pointing in my direction.

Nodding affirmatively, Mr. Wang walked away from Katy and came across the marble lobby toward me. Smiling broadly, as if it were all his own idea, he said that early the next morning, before our tour group left Beijing, he would be very pleased to lead me to the site of one of my parents' former homes.

"You hurry breakfast," he instructed. "Then we walk. Not far. Three four blocks."

A few blocks away?! For three days, that September 1993, I had been pleading with him to tell me how to find one or more of the houses my mother and father had lived in back in the 1920s. He was not impolite, but always dismissive and never informative. Clearly, Katy had insisted that he show me.

After finding her and thanking her profusely for intervening, I marveled over all that had happened that afternoon.

Some people say, *There are no coincidences*. Whether or not that's true, I was deeply grateful that Katy had taken the seat beside me on the bus and noticed the papers on my lap. As soon as she understood that my father had been a respected authority on Asian art, she paid attention to his old photographs showing houses and their addresses in Beijing. She understood how much I'd hoped to see them.

As we later stood in the hotel lobby, she cautioned me. "Keep an open mind, Judy. Things may not look exactly like these pictures. Many years have passed, and the Communists forced a lot of changes." She probably guessed what I would see.

In keeping with his word, Mr. Wang found us at our breakfast table. After rushing us through the meal, the city guide led Ethan and me on a rapid walk through the back streets of Beijing. Unlike the modern boulevards, choked with the flow of bicycles and buses, these streets, called "hutongs," were more like alleys. Formed by the outer walls of the courtyard homes, the narrow passages teemed with early morning activities. People squatted over smoky cooking fires or basins in which they washed their faces or brushed their teeth. Bicycles leaned against every inch of wall space, ready to take their owners off to work or school.

Our guide sprinted along, weaving between pedestrians. It was all we could do to keep him in sight as he ducked into first one turn of a narrow street and then another. Finally, he stopped, pointing with evident satisfaction to an address painted on a wall. As he called out the names of the Chinese characters, we could see that they were identical to the inscription on my father's photographs: "Number two Tung Fu Jia Tao"—the address of a home called "Temple Court," where my parents had lived from April 1926 to October 1927. But instead of being inscribed on the outer wall of an old Chinese dwelling, the large characters stretched vertically down the side of a ten-story concrete building. Although I was disappointed, I wasn't surprised.

I later learned that my parents' old home had been destroyed by the Communists about ten years earlier, during the massive relocation of families from the vast space that was opened to create Tiananmen Square. Tall Soviet-style apartment buildings had been the solution to the problem of where to put the people, and the old one-story structures had to be cleared away to make room.

Ethan and I realized that our guide had known all along that this was what we would find. By ignoring my requests to be directed to this spot the man had not been trying to spare my feelings. Reluctant to hear any resentment we might have voiced about what his government had done, he wanted to spare himself.

We said nothing. He was not responsible. We were still grateful that Katy had persuaded him to bring us to this spot. She knew that we needed to understand.

As we coped with our disappointment, we looked around the neighborhood. Grabbing Ethan's arm, I turned him to see what stood behind him.

"Look! Doesn't that remind you of Ben's photographs?"

In half-destroyed remnants of one of the older homes, we could see the peak of a typical gray tiled roof and the crimson door posts and latticed window frames of openings to an inner courtyard. Corrugated tin fencing and heavy plastic sheeting concealed other portions of the old walls, and from the brick-littered ground we could easily tell that the remains of this once-elegant house were destined to be sacrificed to more "progress."

My father's sister Helen, who had lived with my parents in China for a year, always said that she had no desire to return after the Communist Revolution. She wanted to remember the ancient land as it had been in her youth. Her daughter visited China a few years after Ethan and I were there. Her group was given a tour of some intentionally preserved quadrangle homes.

"You wouldn't have wanted to see them," my cousin Betsy told me. "There were as many as six families crowded into the rooms and living in the courtyard of what would have been a one family home in the 1920s. We saw none of the decorative furnishings and artifacts shown in your dad's photographs. Life was just basic survival inside those old walls."

Although my naïve expectation that I might be able to see a house where my parents had lived was shattered, I was still deeply moved by being able walk where my parents had walked in their early married years. And seeing remnants of one of the old quadrangles helped me to visualize, beyond photos, their home in that ancient city.

Touching my parental roots in that country—at once so foreign and so familiar—evoked in me a sense of completion. I was able to integrate my family legends with the woman I had become. I finally treasured my heritage, knowing how lucky I was to be reared with a sense of a wider world. I could even forgive my younger self for all the years that I had turned my back on it.

When next I talked with Katy Ryor she surprised me again, with a suggestion that led to an astonishing series of events.

3

Katy's Suggestion

"So. How do you feel about what you saw on your morning quest through the old hutongs of Beijing?" asked Katy, the young art historian. Later in the day, we managed to sit together on a domestic flight from Beijing to Xian. As usual, she wore a dark skirt and white blouse, with no concern about varied fashion.

After hearing my emotional account of feeling closer to my parents, seeing a fragment of an old quadrangle, she said, "I've been wondering—do you have any of Benjamin March's papers?"

"Oh yes, almost all, I think. I have six or eight cartons of memorabilia about him. As an only child, I was the designated Keeper of the Flame. You wouldn't believe all the stuff. I not only have albums of photographs Ben took during the two years he lived here, I also have his corresponding diaries. Ethan and I read them before coming to China…"

As Katy's eyes widened, I told her, "I also have extensive lecture notes, and several file boxes full of index cards he used to record his system of symbols." I knew she was aware he devised a way of analyzing the elements of classical scroll paintings.

"Oh gosh!" Katy exclaimed. Responding to her excitement, I confessed that I had sometimes resented the burden of protecting those materials. "There are even flash cards he used while learning Mandarin," I said.

"I've lugged all this stuff from attic to basement to garage, all my adult life. I often wondered what meaning they would ever have to anyone, but I felt duty bound to keep them.

Nodding, Katy looked into my eyes, showing clear understanding. The conversations around us on the small crowded plane sometimes made it difficult to hear each other.

"I particularly wondered about my heirs," I told her, when quiet resumed. I've worried about how my adult children would react when my death hefts this legacy onto their uninformed and presumably unwilling shoulders."

What Katy said next offered an alternative.

"Are you familiar with the Charles Freer Museum and the Arthur M. Sackler Gallery of Art in Washington, D.C.?" she asked. "They are both parts of the Smithsonian..."

Indeed I was, because my college major was art history, and because my father was once awarded a "Freer Fellowship" for research. I knew that Katy was then a Freer Fellow graduate student herself.

"Ah yes, of course!" Katy recalled. "Well, the combined

Freer-Sackler Archive maintains an extensive collection of materials pertaining to Asian art. I am *certain* that they would be delighted to review and possibly receive anything and everything that had been acquired and used by Benjamin March. As I told you yesterday, he is still highly respected for setting standards for the critical examination of Chinese painting."

"That is still astonishing to me," I admitted. I wrote down the name Katy gave me of the curator to contact, pleased by her suggestion but somewhat skeptical. Perhaps Ben's diaries and photos could, as she believed, contribute to a greater body of knowledge about the "Early Sinologists"—as the Westerners who lived and worked in China at the beginning of the 20th Century were called. But, what if she was wrong, and the archivists considered them worthless?

Fearing rejection, I filed away Katy Ryor's information, occasionally mulling over its meaning for me and, potentially for others, but taking no action.

Not then.

But her enthusiasm and conviction caused me to reflect on my father's life and mine.

4

No More Suffers

IT WAS PAST MIDNIGHT when Doré, as I was taught to call my mother, roused me from sleep. Groggily rubbing my eyes, I came awake to a changed house. It was the silence. Even at the age of not-quite six, I knew what that must mean.

"No more suffers," I said.

"Yes, darling," Doré softly replied. "Ben died just a few minutes ago."

For several weeks, she had helped me to understand that the heavy, rasping noises coming from beyond the door into my father's room were caused by his labored breathing.

"His sick heart has gotten larger and larger to try to do its work," she had explained. "It's so big that it is pushing against his lungs and making it hard for him to breathe."

I wasn't quite sure what death was all about, but I had overheard enough whispered conversations to realize that dying would mean a release from suffering.

"Did Ben's heart just get tired of working so hard?" I asked as Doré pulled back my blanket and lifted my pajama-clad body from my bed. "Did it just quit?"

"Yes, Judy Pooh. His poor sick heart finally gave up. Do you want to come with me now and give Ben a kiss to see him on his way?"

Less than six short years—punctuated by his lecture tours, research trips to China and long hours working at the Detroit Institute of Arts or teaching at the University of Michigan—is all I had with my father. But photographs that he took show how closely my Daddy Ben observed me.

My aunt, Lurry, once said, "I thought that you must have been the most photographed child in the world!" Ben even entered enlargements of some portraits in photography exhibitions. Many of what I think of as memories are based on those images or on what Dore told me.

She started at the beginning. A year after their infant son died at birth, she recalled, her husband wanted to try again for a living child. Despite her fears, she agreed, and safely delivered a 9 lb. daughter. They named me Judith.

Ben welcomed his baby girl and took pride as I grew. The lullabies he sang to me at bedtime included favorite cowboy classics such as "Goodbye Old Paint, I'm a-leavin' Cheyenne" and lustily-rendered bawdy ballads such as "Sixteen Men on a Dead Man's Chest. Yo ho ho and a bottle of rum." Little did he know that I envisioned all those drunkards astride some hapless victim's torso rather than a wooden trunk.

Nor did he know how well I had memorized the songs. Shocked teachers at Merrill Palmer Nursery School called my parents in to discuss, with disapproval, the lyrics little Judy used to sing herself to sleep at nap time! Ben and Doré had to avoid each other's eyes to keep from laughing.

When I had the chicken pox, Ben used a watercolor paint brush, dipped in soothing calamine lotion, to paint itch-relieving dot-to-dot pictures on my body.

I remember well the treasures of his study—the Chinese brush holders made of carved ivory and "blood-glaze" pottery; slick black ink stones; small flat porcelain jars of sticky red ink used with carved seals (called "chops") to assert ownership of photographs or scrolls.

No five-year-old had ever received a more wondrous doll house. Painstakingly cut from plywood by Ben, who glued and nailed and painted the 3-ft-tall mansion, it had hand-carved stair railings and a brick-patterned fireplace, doors that swung on hinges and electric ceiling lights in every room. He even created pictures for the walls—out of tiny catalog photos of famous impressionist paintings mounted on cardboard with silver tape frames.

The clear celluloid windows were divided into fourths by slim wooden frames. Doré cut curtains from felt or gingham fabric, as appropriate for each room. She even made wee placemats and napkins for the dining room table and chips of real soap for the bathroom. The miniature wooden appliances mimicked the most up-to-date kitchen equipment. The stove, with its oven raised beside the burners, stood on long, curved legs. A fat, round cooling coil topped the refrigerator. In the living room, a tall radio console and a fern stand joined a grand piano, creating an air of elegance. Ben cut tiny andirons from a metal ruler and snipped white birch twigs that pretended to be logs.

I learned from Doré's letters that Ben liked to tease her for my benefit. When she cleared the table after supper, she used to kiss his hair. He would say, "Gosh, Judy, did you ever hear of a waitress kissing your hair in any other restaurant?" Apparently, I thought this was hilarious. She described how I whispered to him every time she did that, urging him to ask me again, followed by great giggling between me and my daddy.

His favorite breakfast was kippered herrings with scrambled eggs and English muffins with orange marmalade. My mother chose to follow that menu every Christmas morning the rest of her life, and it became a familiar holiday ritual when I prepared those foods for my own family.

"Pentwater Beach: Six rhymes for Judy" is a slim book of poems Ben wrote and illustrated with clever colored drawings evoking my early childhood. He depicted days spent making dribble sand castles on the shore of Lake Michigan near our summer home, himself holding me as he sang by a campfire. The poems descibe my Scotty dog, damp woolen snowsuits in winter and the fairy beams reflected into dark ceiling corners created by Ben as he aimed my mother's hand mirror.

He also cut a flexible wooden switch off a birch tree limb and hung it by the Pentwater fireplace to keep me mindful of his expectations. I can still hear the singing sound it made as he whipped it through the air, but I have no memory of ever feeling its sting.

In 1933, Ben and Doré took me to see the lights and sights of the Chicago World's Fair. All I remember is the miniature souvenir bus. An enlarged photograph Ben took of me playing with the toy is mounted in one of the brocade-covered Chinese-style picture albums called "A Book of Judith." From Doré's letters I learned that my father particularly wanted his little girl to experience that historic assemblage of international exhibitions and enormous carnival attractions. According to her account, I loved the lights.

According to my mother, one night that year, I engaged her in a lengthy conversation about how babies are made. It was probably a successful attempt to keep her at my bedside longer before she declared time for lights out. Ben, she said, was blissfully soaking in a nice hot bath. Not one to postpone reality by telling tales about birds and bees, Doré gave me the anatomical truth. This, she later recalled, prompted an unexpected reaction. I leaped from my bed, dashed down the hall, threw open the bathroom door and demanded, "BEN! LEMME SEE YOUR PENIS!"

The fortuitous timing allowed my astonished father the chance to point wordlessly to the floating culprit. It's my favorite story.

Ben was a Conscientious Objector during World War I. He was conscripted, wore an Army uniform and sent to France. But he was assigned to groom horses in the Cavalry and did not shoot a gun. He urged my mother to make sure that I never played with toy guns. Killing is no game, I learned.

Horses continued to be an important symbol in his life. Ben's last name, in Mandarin Chinese, was "Ma," which, depending on tone, means mother or horse. He collected, and was given, a number of horse figurines, both wooden and pottery, plus miniatures that he displayed on a cabinet that my mother called "the bijoux shelf."

...

The last night before he was confined to bed in the final stage of fatal heart failure, Ben designed a woodblock plate to be pasted in my books. Below the drawing of an adolescent Pilgrim girl of the seventeenth century with a long scarf fluttering out behind her, the legend reads "Judith March Her Book." I was named for that young pioneer. The wife of Hugh March, an inn-keeper in Salem, Massachusetts, that early Judith scandalized the village by wearing a red scarf to church on Sunday. Clearly that iconoclastic gesture appealed to my thoroughly modern parents.

As I followed my mother down the upstairs hallway the night my father died, I padded along with complete confidence in whatever would come next. Doré had never given me any reason to feel squeamish about seeing a dead body.

Sitting beyond the bed was my Granny March. I later learned how glad she was that she had "arrived in time." It didn't occur to me then that the man she was mourning was not just my father. He was her son. At her invitation, I climbed up on Ben's bed, wishing to snuggle into the crook of his sheltering arm as I used to do in the early months of his illness. Quickly, I realized that his rigid body must be what death felt like. But his relaxed face looked peaceful, so I scooched up and kissed his cool cheek.

Then, as Doré reached to lift me down, she asked, "Ready to go back to bed now, Darling?" Seeing my reluctance to leave, she added "I'll come and tuck you in."

Sleepily, I moved slowly through the door.

I don't remember if I asked more questions then. I doubt it. Doré must have looked so tired. Gently, she made it clear that the adults had other tasks to perform, saying, "You can help us by being quiet."

Internalizing an instruction that I later followed in my adult life, I did not cry.

A quiet house meant no more suffers.

5

The Interpreter's Daughter

DURING THE THREE YEARS he lived and taught English in China, my father met and married my mother. They met at one of the frequent gatherings of Western ex-pats. The tall handsome teacher with cropped curly brown hair was immediately attracted to the slim, black-haired woman who had loved the exotic country since her missionary parents took her there as an infant. During their courtship, he also fell in love with Asian art and culture.

The more he learned, the more he dreamed of becoming an "interpreter" of the Far East to Westerners.

"I want Americans to understand and appreciate it as I now do," he explained to family and friends. When, in 1927, Ben was invited to create a Department of Oriental Art at the Detroit Institute of Arts, my parents returned to the United States. He loved the job, and his careful acquisitions earned the department the excellent reputation it maintains today. He traveled often to lecture at other museums across the country.

Meanwhile, Doré hated the "dirty motor city." She had grown up with servants to cook her meals and clean her rooms while she hiked beautiful mountain trails and wrote poetry and children's stories. As a married woman in Michigan, she wondered, "How can any intelligent female settle for the drudgery of housewifely duties?" But she performed the role and became a mother as well.

Due to the Great Depression that followed, the museum had to reduce Ben's job to half time. Fortunately, he was able to accept another part-time position as lecturer on Asian Art at the University of Michigan. When I was four, we moved to Ann Arbor, which offered a cosmopolitan setting for a young family and allowed my father to continue his career.

However, his heart, weakened by scarlet fever in childhood, could not endure the pace of life as he chose to live it. He died at home a few weeks before my sixth birthday. Only gradually did I understand the profound impact it would have on me.

His friends and colleagues all saw his death as a tragic loss. He was not only a brilliant scholar, prominent museum curator, respected author and popular professor; he was a charming, artistic man who was personally admired. Family and friends comforted themselves by reminding my mother that she still had his child.

"At least Ben will live on in Judy," they said.

My parents' decision to limit themselves to one child was made with poignant awareness that his serious heart condition would almost surely cause an early death, and that Doré would become a single parent.

So, she became the regent for her six-year-old heir apparent, and my role in life was to assume the mantle of "Ben March's daughter." Living up to that heritage meant not simply academic achievement but perfection in every way.

When I excelled at school or was well behaved, she told me "Daddy Ben is so proud of you." Not that he *would be* proud of me if he were alive, but that he *was* proud of me. And if she thought that I was being lazy or disobedient, then it was "Daddy Ben is very disappointed in you."

The catch was that I couldn't defend myself. Godlike, Ben would zap down from heaven to pass judgment on me and then whisk up and away again, leaving me with my guilt and remorse for being less than perfect.

I tried very hard to earn his approval and make him proud. Academically, I initially followed in his footsteps. But, unconsciously, I developed a quiet resentment of the towering standards imposed by my "Father in Heaven." At 21, I turned my back on my heritage, married a fruit grower and moved to a farm.

I was past 40 before I understood that my father was not the one who held unrealistic expectations. It was my *mother* who created the myth of Almighty Ben.

In her youth, Doré had adored travel and longed for a carefree life of exotic adventures. Before Ben died, he asked her to promise that I would be educated in America. For them, "educated" meant a college degree. Without that pledge, he knew, her immediate response to his death would be, as she later told a friend, "to tuck the child under my arm and flee home to China."

Thus, to raise Ben March's daughter, Doré had to give up her private dreams. She needed to own my legacy in order to justify the sacrifices she made to keep that deathbed promise. And I never felt quite good enough to lift the sadness from her eyes.

It is intriguing to imagine how our lives might have unfolded if she had followed her own desires, but I can't second-guess her decision. Although she freely chose her course, I understand how trapped she felt. I have long since forgiven her.

When I finally visited China in 1993, experiences there opened me to an appreciation of my heritage.

馬

BOOK TWO

Latchkey Kids

"Child of self forever free
stay with me eternally.
Excite my soul, laugh and leap
and in my heart I will keep
your sweet joy of innocence.
From all shadow of pretense
Lead me to your world of play
share with me a carefree day."

– Norman Olsson

1

Whispering Years

"Yeeeowww!" Patsy wailed. "STOP Mama! Puh-leeezzz!! Oowwwch!"

But on and on went the ritual—Tug—Scream—"Hold still, Patricia!"—Tug—Scream. "Hold STILL, I tell you! The more you wiggle, the longer this will take!"

For the last half hour before school every morning the whole house rang with wailing, as Marjorie tugged the snarls out of each small section of her daughter's springy hair before winding it around her finger and letting it fall into a perfect shiny coil. Finally, with some two dozen golden ringlets artfully arranged above her damp-eyed face, Patsy emerged to stomp down the stairs and scuff off to school with me.

After my father's death, Doré, could no longer afford to keep the large house on Morton Avenue. Fortunately, she was able to rent an attractive two-bedroom apartment that suited our needs. Ideally located, it was four blocks from the university campus, where my mother was given a job as librarian in the Department of the History of Art. And six blocks in the opposite direction was Eberbach Elementary School where I entered second grade.

For the following six years, this apartment was the crucible where I learned the need to be a perfect child in order to live up to the honor of being Ben March's daughter. Additionally, I learned the give and take of having one daily playmate.

The top two floors of a three-story white frame house at 612 Church Street was divided into two spacious apartments. The apartment rented by Patsy Johnstone and her mother Marjorie was a mirror image of ours, with entry doors just a narrow hallway apart at the top of the front stairway. Our landlords occupied the ground floor.

For the next six years, Patsy and I were as tightly wound as her Shirley Temple curls. We were the same age and in the same grade in school, but beyond that we couldn't have been more different. Petite and adorable, Patsy operated with a calculated cuteness that endeared her to adults and kept me enslaved. Years of hearing and sometimes witnessing the torture that produced those Hollywood ringlets never diminished my envy of those curls!

After school, until 5 o'clock, we were "latchkey kids." In the 1930s, schools did not provide programs to shelter and entertain children whose parents held fulltime jobs. We were expected to go home, let ourselves in, and amuse and behave ourselves on our own. In our case, the landlady, Mrs. Kempf was usually at home, and Patsy's Grandma Maleaux was across the hall, but the women were oblivious to whatever two trustworthy little girls were doing in my bedroom.

Actually, the only way that we even flirted with danger was when I rode my trusty stallion, which was really a railing that ran from the top of our interior staircase, for a few feet along the upstairs hall.

I was the cowboy, of course. Taller and huskier than Patsy, I always had to be the cowboy or the prince, while she got to be Cinderella, Sleeping Beauty or Snow White. Occasionally I would question the casting. The 1937 Disney "Snow White" Halloween costume had a yellow apron designed to go over the red skirt. I remember tying the apron around my head, babushka fashion, to pretend that I had long golden hair.

"Let ME be the princess this time!" I would plead.

"No!" asserted Patsy, "It just wouldn't be right. You're the biggest. You have to be the boy."

Although I wouldn't have acknowledged any resentment then, I internalized the message: my size was unfeminine, which eventually translated into undesirable.

Besides dress-up and make-believe, we played with doll babies, stuffed animals, and the miniature family that lived in the detailed wooden doll house my father had built for me. The scenarios were always dictated by my constant companion.

In dry, clear weather, we would roller skate to school and back. Platform skates were strapped to our shoes and attached to the soles with clamps that tightened with a skate key. To safeguard this necessity, we kids wore the hexagonal tube-like tool on a ribbon or cord around our necks.

Our grade school did not have a cafeteria, so Patsy carried a lunch packed by her grandmother. Students who lived near enough to eat at kitchen tables walked home at noon. No one noticed where I went.

A drug store, about two blocks beyond the schoolyard's chain link fence, had a lunch counter in the rear. Doré established an account there. So Monday through Friday I perched on one of five high silvery metal stools with round red leather tops, and ordered a cheeseburger. My beverage was a chocolate milk shake and dessert was a frozen Milky Way bar retrieved from the stash that Andy, the counter man, kept for me. No wonder I was chubby.

Every Saturday night, "Foxy Grandpaw" made me feel very special.

When my mother and I ate Chinese food in our favorite booth at the Lantern Gardens, this frail old man came out of his kitchen to fuss over the little blue-eyed girl who had learned to use chopsticks before a knife and fork.

There it was even polite to chew the tangy pork off a bitesize sparerib and spit out the smooth clean bone. I liked green pepper tomato beef the best, but whether shrimp or chicken or pea pods or cabbage, whatever went into my bowl had to be eaten. As I was oft reminded, "Every grain of rice left in your bowl will be a pock mark on your grandchildren." Since today my children's children have clear complexions, I feel amused pride over my obedience—never mind vaccinations.

Walking home from the restaurant, along the Michigan campus retail core on State Street, we stopped to buy my next morning's breakfast of chocolate walnut Mary Lee fudge. I happily carried the one-pound box as we continued on the "diag"—shorthand for the long broad pedestrian way that crossed the campus diagonally.

Our Sunday morning routine was inviolate. Doré slept late. I was not allowed to wake her til noon. The fudge bribe, washed down with grenadine flavored ginger ale, kept me quiet. That and fear. I couldn't risk rousing her—no matter what—because to incur her icy disappointment or disapproval would mean extending my loneliness into a long silent afternoon.

My mother deserved that one day of sleep. I knew that well. She had to go to work every other day—often even Saturday mornings. And she did all that for me—to buy my clothes and food and pay the rent on our attractive apartment near her on campus office. Her whole life was sacrificed for me. The least I could do was keep out of her sight week nights and let her sleep till noon on Sundays.

So—between my sixth and twelfth years of age I never questioned my confinement to a large bedroom that was both sanctuary and prison without bars. I didn't envy my friends who had to go to Sunday school to be indoctrinated with religion, which my mother haughtily dismissed as "a crutch for the weak."

My security was found in books. Companioned in the early years by Pooh and Piglet, I later lived with fictional friends in Lapland or Czechoslovakia, or Germany or the Netherlands.

On the wall over my bed a large illustrated map of "The Land of Make Believe" traced paths through welcoming woods to such charmed destinations as Sleeping Beauty's castle and the tower of the little lame prince. Behind closed eyes tonight I can see the nursery rhyme characters along the way—Jack and Jill, the Crooked Man and Little Miss Muffet eternally springing away from the spider beside her. I spent hours creating my own adventures along those painted paths and streams.

When homework banished Patsy and me to separate bedrooms in the evening, we developed a secret way to communicate. Years earlier, when the house had been divided, a long upstairs hall had been blocked in the middle by a Masonite partition. One side of it formed the back of Patsy's clothes closet. The other side was concealed behind a Chinese mirror at the end of my hallway. Once we discovered this flimsy barrier, we began a nightly ritual of whispering between our apartments. Usually, the content of our clandestine conversations was nothing more interesting than the answers to homework problems, or whether the cutest boy in class had looked at Patsy in school.

Sometimes we talked about our mothers. They were as different as their daughters. Marjorie was Wonder Bread. Doré was a hand-painted Chinese fan. Marjorie rarely read. Doré was seldom without a book. Marjorie's divorce soured her on all men. Doré had many admirers. I was accustomed to having them around, but it was still quite startling when I surprised a naked man in our bathroom early one Sunday morning.

"You must be Judy," he said cheerfully, as he covered himself with a towel around his waist. Gulping assent, I rapidly retreated and ran back upstairs.

Patsy's grandmother discovered the secret communication going on at the back of the clothes closet and persuaded Marjorie to forbid it. Despite our bitter complaints, my pal and I soon outgrew those whispering years. When something BIG happened, we could speak of it openly.

Just before my twelfth birthday, my mother remarried. Don Goss (the nude bather) moved in with us. He was friendly to me, without paying special notice. Perhaps he knew that one of Doré's earlier lovers had tried courting the child as a way of impressing the mother. Big Mistake. She was not one to share a man's attention, even with her own daughter.

But, when Don helped me with arithmetic or gave me his opinion on the way my dress or hair looked, she gladly relinquished some parenting responsibilities. Relaxing into the role of wife again, she was assured that Don's masculine hand would help smooth my transition into adolescence. The three of us looked forward to a cozy family life.

When that did not come about, one of the ways my life changed was the end of daily connection with Patsy Johnstone.

2

Pentwater

"OH JUDY, I can *smell* Lake Michigan!" Doré would always say, long before we saw it.

The drive north from Ann Arbor every June lifted the curtain on our annual summer vacation. As pine trees began to replace oaks and maples along the two-lane U.S. 31 beyond Muskegon, we could catch brief glimpses of sand dunes to the west between the small towns of Whitehall, Montague and Hart.

Finally, we would come to Pentwater Lake, commonly called "the Little Lake." Then, soon, when the pavement turned left, we would draw closer to the sharp right turn that became Hancock Street—"the main drag"—of the resort village of Pentwater.

I didn't envy classmates who spent two weeks crammed in a car going to see Mount Rushmore or Old Faithful. If anything, they envied my spending three months at a "summer cottage." I'll always be grateful that Doré's choice to work a nine-month academic schedule and her solid year-round money management made possible our full summers in her beloved retreat near the shores of Lake Michigan.

Our place on an interior street of the village was not a "cottage." It was an old, traditional house that Doré remodeled and redecorated. Although we, too, were considered "resorters," we were not among those who used the word *summer* as a verb. We hardly knew the wealthy people who owned posh vacation homes on the South Beach, with broad decks facing sunsets over "The Big Lake." Years later, I married into a family that owned two modest cottages on the less prestigious North Beach, but that's another story.

Between the two stretches of homes ran the Charles Mears State Park. Uniformed employees maintained a long expanse of wide "singing sand" beach plus a bathhouse and small store, which stocked sundries for campers and candy for kids.

My mother and I spent every afternoon at that beach. I could wake her when the noon siren rang out from the village fire station. Then I would clamber up beside her in the Ford coupe, laden with towels, old blankets, magazines for her and sand pails and shovels for me. She doubtless had a sunscreen lotion in her beach bag, although we both acquired tawny tans by September. The route to the beach ran about ten blocks from our house to the State Park. I walked it often as I grew up.

Joining us would be my best friend Bobby Hueseman and his mother Brenzelle. "Bren," was a divorcée from Springfield, Illinois, who rented a small house for the whole summer. She and Doré probably met on the beach—both preferring to spread their blankets far north, away from ordinary tourists.

She and her little boy, who was just my age, were our constant companions over many summers. Often, after supper together, Bobby would fall asleep at our house while the two women talked—and drank—into the night. Bren, tall and stout, chose beer. Doré whose lithe figure was flattered by Chinese silk robes, favored rye whiskey with water.

They never considered not taking the children to the beach every day, unless heavy rain drenched the plan. Then Bobby and I ran toy cars on the patterned "streets" of our dining room linoleum, instead of in the vast cities we created on the sand. In later years, we competed with other friends for Monopoly money at the dining room table.

...

The highlight of every year was when my unmarried aunt, Lurry, came from Manhattan to spend her two-week vacation with us. Not only did she and Doré cherish each other as sisters, they were best friends who never ran out of conversation.

For me, Lurry was an ideal companion. She got up early and spent time with me while Doré slept in 'til noon. Lurry led me over the dunes on long hikes which Doré was denied by ill health. The attributes of the two women complemented each other, such that they formed, in my mind and heart, two halves of one perfect mother.

Another visitor during my childhood was Doré's father, Grandaddy Rowe. The two adored each other and cherished the vacation time together. Sweet, courtly, with white hair and matching goatee, he used a cane to support a leg damaged by a stroke. Several times, he took Bobby and me to an early movie.

Much as I loved the dear old man, I was embarrassed by his barking laughter in the film's comic moments.

When I was a teenager, Pentwater's business district extended three blocks, from the Dairy Queen, on the corner of the beach road, to the Dairy Bar Restaurant, where I eventually held my first job. The post office was on the same side of the street as Meyers' Market and Elwin Kent's Funeral Home across from Mrs. Worrell's corner Antiques Shop and the dry goods store. In later years, Mrs. Worrell sold out to the Gustafsons, who created a two-level wonderland of souvenirs and imported treasures.

Next to the movie theater was a wide green city park, centered by a white-painted band stand where local musicians played Sousa marches and old show tunes every Thursday evening. At least four generations of appreciative listeners sat blanket-to-blanket on the gentle grassy slope that descended from the sidewalk to a flat lawn. Everyone knew each other's babies as they crawled across extended adult legs in search of forbidden treats. Older folk set up haphazard rows of folding chairs and sent some big kids to fetch bulbous double-dip ice cream cones from The Bakery across the street. The village park was also the venue for arts and crafts fairs on summer Saturdays.

The Bakery reeked of greasy soups and meatloaf dinners but also drew us in for soft cinnamon rolls and enormous raisin cookies that I can taste in memory. Today, a jillion T-shirt stores and cutesy giftee shoppees line the street, but, as in most tourist towns, the bars survived.

Of the three, the Antler Bar always outdrew its rivals—famed not only for its juicy world-class hamburgers with thick slices of sweet onion, but for the stability of its clientele. Louie Maynard and Charlie Daggett, pillars of the postal service, could always be found bellied up under the huge antlers of stags' heads high on the walls, along with realtors Harold Shaw and Cook Richmond plus other village characters. Every noon, card games picked up where the hands had folded the day before.

As self-appointed monitors of everyone's business, the men rivaled any sewing circle in their attention to the details of village life. When I went to the post office, Charlie might ask me, "How long's your mother's sister gonna be here from Noo York this year?"

"I see you got a letter from your uncle over there on Taiwan!" Louie would marvel, nearly drooling for a peek at the exotic missive.

The movie theater stopped running films around 1960. Not showing a profit, I guess. It's an office building now. I always hoped some entrepreneur would open it up to show movies again, at least in the summer when "the resorters" and "the boaters" took over the town.

Pentwater appeals to the boating crowd because of its sheltered harbor on Pentwater Lake. Long before my own time, the village evolved as a logging port—a thriving commercial hub safely "pent in by water."

Early in my lifetime, lumber barges were replaced by sailboats and yachts that arrived through The Channel which connects this so-called "Little Lake" to the "Big Lake"—Lake Michigan. Four city blocks long and wider than an Olympic pool, the Channel challenged swimmers, including my aunt Lurry, who last stroked across it in her seventy-second year.

This striking access between lakes still attracts boaters from as far away as Chicago. When not a destination, Pentwater makes a perfect stopover on a long sail to Traverse City, Petoskey, Charlevoix or Mackinac Island.

The massive concrete piers weren't constructed until I was about twelve or thirteen. I know it wasn't much later than that, because I still have a snapshot of me at fourteen, seated there with long tanned legs stretched out in a pose evocative of Lana Turner or Ava Gardner. As a young child, I loved to play in spaces between rotting wood timbers of the old pier. Filled with sand washed in by each storm, these cubicles, about six feet square, could be forts, humble huts or secret chambers, depending on our imaginations. Bobby and I were hidden there, we thought, until, on very windy days, our mothers huddled in with us to escape the sting of blowing sand. Sometimes, the women would drag their blankets and gear to deep dugouts high in the dunes. Those hollows also offered warmth as our beaching days stretched into September.

...

In my childhood, Pentwater's residential streets were still rutted, either slimy mud or dry dirt that blew in through the screen door with every passing Ford or Chevy. I can remember the excitement when asphalt surfacing was added. Earlier, I pressed my small footprint in the wet concrete of curbing that still marks the front boundary of the lot at 78 N. Wythe Street.

I went barefoot ALL summer. The only time I wore sandals was the one evening when Lurry took us out for dinner at "The Jenny Wren," the only upscale restaurant in town.

In my early childhood, the narrow side street between our house and the Nelsons' was coated with cinders to keep down dust. In June, I would wince and squeal as I gingerly picked my way across to visit—and wince and squeal back home. By the Fourth of July, my feet would be toughened up enough to scurry across without complaint, and by the end of August, the calluses would be so thick that I could stroll with total nonchalance. One September, when I was starting third grade back in Ann Arbor, I walked off barefoot for the first day of school. Apparently, Dore didn't notice. Her job at the university hadn't resumed yet, so she was probably still in summer mode, too. She had to take notice when the teacher sent me home in disgrace. "Never let your child come without shoes again."

...

Memories of Pentwater shift and overlap like advancing and receding waves on the sandy shore. I think of waking up to the distinctive cooing of mourning doves and hearing the raucous shriek of gulls as fishing boats entered the channel. I can conjure the scent of sun-baked skin on my arm and, years later, on the bodies of my freckled children. I think of the taste of fresh raspberries on Rice Krispies and of Doré's celebrated chili con carne. When Bobby and I begged to stay longer by the water some late afternoons, she would drive home to get a pot of chili and bring it to the beach at sunset for supper around a campfire.

Lurry and I often ate breakfast on the small back terrace outside the kitchen. Looking beyond a low red brick wall bordering the cement floor, we could survey our wide back yard.

A magnificent blue spruce towered over the jack pines and junipers that screened the Freelands' dark barn behind our lot. The back terrace was also a favorite spot for the adults' cocktails with frequent houseguests from Detroit or Ann Arbor.

In 1932, Doré hired a gardener to plant a long row of small cedar trees along the side of her newly-acquired property. Over the next dozen years, they grew into a dense hedge, about ten feet high. It afforded complete privacy on that side of the yard. An opening, almost obscured by then, had once lined up exactly with the side door of our friends' screened-in porch, two lots away. When the Nelsons built a tennis court on the lot between our houses, that congruence no longer gave me a shortcut. Their tall wire mesh fence kept balls inside and little girls out. I had to walk around it.

Inside our vacation house, a wide white brick fireplace dominated the living room. I can picture pale birch logs stacked to the left. On the right hung a string of Mexican clay banks, crafted to look like a variety of fruits. Children could put pennies in the slots, but were warned that they could never get them out. Embroidered white Numdah rugs offered softness and warmth on the wooden floors. Every floor in the house was painted blue. The shade that might be called a royal or sailor blue came to be known as "Doré blue" to family and friends.

Long burlap draperies hung beside the two tall living-room windows. Painted with realistic pine trees by my father, they were a conversation piece throughout my childhood. Sometime in the 1950s, my mother decided to let in more light and replaced them with pale blue sheers. *(My husband and I soon used the burlap draperies to artfully conceal laundry equipment in our basement recreation room.*

Some thirty years later, it was touching to see that he had saved them, after our divorce, and installed Ben March's creations as a room divider in a cottage he and his brothers inherited from his aunt.)

Off the living room, directly inside the front door, stood a small bedroom that Daddy Ben used as his "study." No one ever studied in there after he died, but his huge Chinese desk continued to dominate the room and the space was forever called by that name. On a long, table-high wooden case, which held the complete set of bound Encyclopedia Britanica, stood a wind-up Victrola, on which my father played records of both Mozart symphonies and cowboy songs. When I received the gift of an electric "vic" with automatic player device, I could stack a whole album of vinal versions of popular music and the classical music I had learned to love.

Bookcases and old steamer trunks lined the rest of the study walls. The room never lost its distinctive musty, even slightly moldy smell from being closed and shuttered with the rest of the house all winter. My adult children can conjure that odor in their sensory memories to this day.

The only exception to Dore's blue floors was in the kitchen, where the plain lumpy surface was painted dark red. When I recall the inconvenient layout of that room, with no counter space and the refrigerator hidden in a separate pantry, I still marvel at the masterful meals my mother produced. My job, after drying the dishes, was to carry them to a china closet in the dining room under the stairs.

From the large central dining room, the tall stairway rose to the second floor. The bannister, like all the woodwork, was painted a soft rosy hue. Doré said she picked a color that would complement any shade of gladiola blooms. On the edges of the stair steps my mother placed Fiesta Ware tumblers filled with orange and yellow marigolds or red and pink zinnias.

Although Doré loved to raise these annuals in flower beds along the side of the house, she never encouraged me to so much as plant a petunia. Moreover, although she loved to cook, she never taught me to fry an egg. In retrospect, that fills me with regret. I wonder if *once,* as a child, I declined an opportunity to learn, thereby forfeiting any further chances. Maybe she never wanted to be bothered. That's probable.

Upstairs, each bedroom was decorated in a different color. Doré's was Wedgewood blue, my aunt Lurry's pale yellow and mine moss green. In each room was a tiny dressing table—a popular "do-it-yourself" variety. Doré covered the kidney-shaped wooden top of each one with cloth in keeping with the room's color scheme. To conceal the spindly legs, she sewed skirts of coordinated calico. Wooden arms supporting the skirts parted in front to allow access to small drawers for hairbrushes, bobby pins and curlers. She painted small wooden benches to match. To store our shorts and T-shirts, she scrounged old chests of drawers at yard sales and auctions. These she also painted to match each room's décor.

In the antique bathroom, where the porcelain sink was set into a square slab of marble, the deep tub stood off the floor on four clawed feet—painted blue.

In addition to the living room fireplace, another heart of the home was the "jazz couch" in the dining room. The broad daybed, built into a corner opposite the stairs, consisted of a full-size mattress set on a wooden platform in a box-like frame edged with paneling painted to match the rest of the rosy woodwork.

Covered with a woven Russian bedspread and cornered with a dozen small bright throw pillows, it was in constant use. It was a spot for children to read, play dolls or tumble; a place for guests to flop after one of Doré's bountiful beef Stroganoff or lamb curry dinners. In future summers, the jazz couch was the center of my world as I recovered from long illness and was courted by my future husband.

From my perspective now, I can't imagine how my life would have unfolded without Pentwater summers.

3

Glen Ellyn

DURING THE SUMMER of 1938, my mother felt tired most of the time, lacking her usual pep. She was not just fashionably slim, but thin to the point of emaciation. In September, when we returned to Ann Arbor from the long school vacation on Lake Michigan, she submitted to a hospital stay for medical testing.

Dr. Marianna Smalley, our beloved family physician, gave her the resulting diagnosis. "Doré," she said, "it turns out that you have diabetes. It isn't life-threatening, but it is a severe illness. And, in an adult-onset case like yours, it will be life-changing."

As Doré struggled to grasp the meaning of this news, she gradually understood that, with treatment, she would eventually get back to a normal life. But first, she would have to stay in the hospital for some six weeks of bed rest.

"But that's impossible," she blurted. "I have to work! And what about Judy? Who can take care of Judy?"

A lucky coincidence soon eased her mind. My late father's parents, Granny and Granddaddy March, were scheduled to stop by Ann Arbor after a driving trip that very week. The timing allowed them to be in on a conference with the doctor. As soon as they heard the dilemma, they offered a solution.

"We will take Judy home with us tomorrow," said Granny. "And she can stay just as long as necessary."

When Granddaddy assured her of his agreement, Doré gratefully accepted. So it was decided. Doré would enter the hospital. Our little black Scotty dog, Sandy, would go into a kennel, and I would spend the first semester of fifth grade in Glen Ellyn, Illinois.

Although my mother was gravely ill when admitted to St. Joseph's, injections of insulin and a diet of high carbohydrate foods soon had her gaining weight. With this treatment, plus much-needed rest, she soon felt more alive than she had for months. In a few weeks, she was allowed to return to our apartment, but she continued on leave from her University of Michigan job for the entire first semester.

Meanwhile, at the age of nine, I was adjusting to strict household expectations. In my grandparents' home, my preferences in foods were not indulged. I was expected to eat whatever was set before me—and all of it. I stayed chubby. The household must be quiet in the evening so that Granddaddy could concentrate on his reading. Bedtime was not negotiable.

But my tall, elegant Grandmother was unfailingly kind. At one cozy end of the long master bedroom she taught me to knit, sew simple doll clothes, and darn socks. I treasured our conversations punctuated by lessons such as, "Only a lazy tailor uses long lengths of thread, Judy. See how your thread has knotted again? Cut it about in half before you continue. You might have to measure out another length before you're done, but it will save time in the long run." Granny's sweet understanding of my feelings eased the loneliness I experienced apart from my mother.

My assigned room was the opposite corner of the large golden stucco house. I remember lying on the carpet while cutting up old Sears Roebuck catalogs to make clothes for paper dolls. I also drew clothes for a doll I designed. The closet in that room fascinated me. When the mirrored bi-fold doors were opened at a certain angle, my image was repeatedly reflected, seemingly to an infinite degree. Creating that illusion was a favorite pastime.

Loretta, a buxom laundress who came in once a week, was happy to have a little girl's company while she ironed. She also helped me with my homework, reaching her shiny mahogany-hued arm down over my shoulder to point out the next step in some pesky long division problem. The strong scent of Fels Naphtha soap always reminds me of those companionable late afternoons.

I walked to school and stayed over the noon hour. A woman who lived across the street from the school provided hot lunches in her home for several students who lived too far away to get home and back in time. My grandparents must have paid her, but such details didn't enter my mind at the time.

The latest rage among the fifth-grade girls in Illinois was collecting pairs of playing cards. They were collected for the pictures on the backs, not the numbers on the faces.

New cards were usually boxed in pairs, with the two decks printed in contrasting colors. Our goal was to amass as many pairs as possible, but cuteness counted. The most popular pictures for trading were cuddly kittens, frisky puppies or Scotty dogs. Ordinary scrollwork designs weren't even considered. Romanticized scenes of hoop-skirted ladies with parasols were also favored, along with curly haired young women flying high on flower-bedecked swings. Kids begged adults for the jokers or instruction cards from new decks, or other cards not needed for rummy, bridge or canasta.

My grandparents' standards differed sharply from Dore's liberal views. The generational contrast caused me some grief when one tearful struggle concerned my underwear.

Granddaddy was offended when my nine-year-old thighs were exposed as I sat wide-legged playing jacks on the living room floor. He insisted that I be made to wear knee-length knit bloomers instead of my customary cotton briefs.

I begged to be able to call Doré about this grossly unfair imposition of old fashioned values. "PLEASE tell Granny that I don't have to wear them," I pleaded on the phone.

"Judy, it will only be for a couple of months, and if it keeps things smooth with Granny and Granddaddy, you can do it," Doré said.

"Well, I know I can if I have to," I acknowledged, "but you should SEE these things! They are hot and itchy and none of the other girls have to wear such awful old things!"

"I know, Sweetie, but if it really matters to Granddaddy and he and Granny are being so good to have you there, it's little enough for you to do to please them, don't you think?"

"Oh I suppose so," I grumbled.

"That's my good girl," said Dore, relieved. "Now, put Granny on the phone so I can tell her I will pay for buying the bloomers."

...

By Christmastime, Dore had gained 20 pounds and was able to stop consuming a daily pint of whipping cream and quarter pound of butter. Her doctors were happy that she had reached the goal of weighing 129, and she certainly felt healthier. The new diet was less complicated and easier to maintain, so she was actually hungry before meals. Weighing her food on a little gram scale had become automatic.

When she arrived in Glen Ellyn for the holidays, Doré learned that I had not believed my grandparents' assurances about her health and was terrified that my mother was going to die. They told her that I had even had nightmares about it. That may have been an exaggeration. I don't remember feeling such terror. But fear would have been understandable, just three years after my father's death.

In a letter to her sister Lurry, Doré wrote, "Even now Judy will touch me or kiss my hand and say, 'Oh Doré, I'm so glad you're alive.'"

She decided to take me back to Ann Arbor after Christmas, even though the school semester in Glen Ellyn didn't end until late January. Whatever discrepancy that created didn't seem to matter to my old elementary school, and I resumed studies with my former classmates. Thanks to Loretta, I was even ahead of them in long division.

4

Poppy

MY NEW STEPFATHER, Don Goss, was as handsome as Clark Gable. He had even played small parts in Hollywood movies before we met him. Sometimes I felt proud of that. Sometimes it embarrassed me. He had always been what was then called "a playboy," —a rich man's son who never thought much about getting a real job until, at the age of 36, he fell in love with a widow who had a half-grown child.

He and my mother, Doré, married two weeks before my 12th birthday. Six years had passed since my father's death, so family and friends were happy for her. I was too, to the limited extent that I understood why she needed a new husband. Don certainly wouldn't have been my choice. He was friendly enough, but he didn't pay as much attention to *me* as one of her former lovers had. Dore believed that her own happiness would make her a better mother and lead to my well-being in the long run. Her happiness had always mattered to me because she was all I had. When she was sad, in her quiet, dry-eyed way, my heart ached too. So, I grudgingly accepted her choice for our futures.

After their brief honeymoon in Chicago, Don Goss moved into our apartment. Doré went back to work at the University of Michigan, I went back to school, and Don drove to his office job with an advertising firm in Detroit. He and I eased into our new relationship with every expectation of having years of family life ahead.

Suddenly, three months later, that dream was totally disrupted: Doré was diagnosed with severely advanced Tuberculosis. Doctors ordered complete bed rest at the state TB sanatorium and warned that a cure could take many months. Late one night, before she had to be admitted, I overheard a frantic discussion about what to do with me.

"Oh my god, Doré," Don stammered, "Judy's a good kid, but how in the world.... How can I *possibly* take care of her by myself?"

"No, Darling. Of course you can't." Doré said soothingly. "This is all so overwhelming. And I feel so lousy....I just can't think."

"Oh Sweet, don't fret," he assured her, surely terrified of losing her to this life-threatening illness. "I will manage somehow...."

The next day, Doré told me that she had decided to ask my paternal grandparents if I could go to live with them in Glen Ellyn, Illinois. Surprised to hear that I had to live *anywhere* else, I begged to stay in Ann Arbor. I had spent six months with Granny and Granddaddy March when I was nine—when Doré was quite ill with acute diabetes. They doted on me then, but their old-fashioned ideas and limited stamina made it less than ideal either for them or for me.

"Oh pleaaeese, Doré!" I cried, "Remember how Granddaddy made Granny buy me knee-length bloomers so he couldn't see up my legs under my dresses?"

"Yes, of course," she said crisply. "But you and Don can't stay here alone."

"Yes we can!" I interrupted. "I will be *really* good and help out. I can learn to cook...and everything—"

"Oh, Judy...Be sensible."

I tried another tack, wailing, "But going to Glen Ellyn would mean leaving all my friends...and my school..."

"Stop it! I just don't see any other choice..."

Don's widowed mother, Gertrude Goss, came to the rescue. She invited him to bring me to live in the large white mansion on the outskirts of Ann Arbor, where he had grown up. Don's sister, Dorothy, who at 40 was considered an old maid, still lived there, as did his 28-year-old bachelor brother Kelly.

"I am so grateful to them all," Doré wrote to her sister Lurry. "And so relieved about Judy's care. I can now accept my fate and enter the san."

Don then faced the task of giving up the apartment and putting all our belongings, including antique Chinese furnishings and artifacts, into commercial storage or his mother's basement.

"He was simply amazing," Doré told Lurry. "He was so calm and sure and cheerful, and none of the messy details stopped him at all."

One messy detail was my Scotty dog. Because the Goss household included Kelly's two large Dalmatians, it seemed unfair to add an aging scotch terrier. So Don took on the sad task of having Sandy put to sleep. Heartbroken when I learned what had happened, I yelled at him, "Why didn't you TELL me?"

"Because I knew you would cry, like you are now." Don said.

"But you didn't even let me say goodbye," I sobbed.

"I guess I thought it would be easier if you didn't know ahead... Maybe that was wrong... I'm sorry...I know you'll miss Sandy..." His voice trailed off as I stomped upstairs to throw myself on the bed. Although Don and Doré undoubtedly made the decision together, I held it against my new stepfather. But not for long.

Although Don and Doré lived together for only three months, hospital visits were like chaperoned dates. His devotion did not wane. Don demonstrated his commitment to Doré in the way he rose to the challenge of parenting her daughter. If his family marveled at his newfound maturity, I was unaware of that at the time.

After we were settled at Skylodge, Don came up with enticing Saturday outings for the two of us. He taught me to ice skate at the indoor city arena, making me believe that it was as much fun for him as for me. He took me horseback riding at a nearby stable and was willing to repeat both of these activities frequently. In her letters to me, Doré had started referring to Don by the Japanese honorific "Papa San." As his devotion to her extended to me, I nicknamed him Poppy.

Poppy knew he was good looking and he loved to flirt. Once, when he drove me to a junior high school dance, he parked and walked into the gym with me instead of dropping me off at the door. It was okay at first, as he stood chatting with my homeroom teacher, Miss Reid. But, when the music started up again and he asked her to dance, I silently willed myself to wake up from this nightmare. Fortunately, he noticed my distress. Sensitive to my embarrassment, he excused himself from his partner, gave me a squeeze around my shoulders and took off, leaving me to hear the giggles of my starry-eyed girlfriends. I don't think that my teacher came down to earth the rest of the evening.

Don's bedroom and mine were across the hall from each other. He always responded cheerfully to my knock and willingly helped me with my homework or offered his opinion on which blouse looked best with the skirt I planned to wear.

One morning, before he was fully dressed, I surprised him with a most unusual appeal. In the bathroom earlier I had realized that my first menstrual period had started. I knew what was happening, but not what to do about it. Not wanting to be a nuisance, but needing help, I tapped gently on Poppy's door.

"Doré told me what to expect," I assured him. "But I don't have any pads or anything…"

Don's reaction was all I could ask for. He quickly pulled on his clothes, jumped in the car, drove into town and gallantly shopped for Kotex and a sanitary belt.

"Here ya go, Kiddo," he said on his return. "There's a picture on the box…Can you see how to hook things together?"

"I think I can figure it out," I responded, from my new level of maturity.

After I was trussed up to meet the world again, Poppy wrote some magnificent lie to excuse my being late for school.

Reflecting today on how he handled the whole situation, I must say he went beyond the call of duty for any father, much less a new stepfather.

About a year after I had moved to Skylodge, I was given some surprising news: I would be allowed to visit my mother who was, by then, a patient in the University Hospital. I had not been permitted to see her in all those long months that she was forty miles away at the TB sanatorium, and not even when she was first moved to Ann Arbor, so the prospect of a visit was really exciting—and it was to be that very day!

When my new Aunt Dorothy Goss picked me up after school, she seemed distracted, but could not explain the sudden permission.

Doré's bed had been wheeled to a bright sun porch. Surprised and thrilled, I assumed that meant we could talk by ourselves. Her damp, hollow eyes told me there was more to it.

First she explained, "You have to stay over on that side of the room, Judy—to make sure you don't catch TB. We aren't allowed to touch each other..."

Then, quickly, she went on to say that she had begged her doctors to let her be the one to tell me some sad news. My Poppy had been in an early morning accident on his way to work.

"His car skidded off the icy road," she said. "It hit a tree. He was killed instantly......."

"Killed?" I needed to hear that word again.

"Yes, Darling..." Doré rushed on. "They say that he died on the impact and wouldn't have suffered at all."

Oh, how I wanted to cross that wide room and climb up on my mother's bed to hold and be held. I had come to love my Poppy so much and could no longer imagine my young life without him. Even as I struggled to understand what this cruel blow of fate would mean for my own future, I saw that tears were filling my mother's eyes again.

My words reflected the way that I had been raised. "Don't you dare cry, Doré. Gosh, that would kill Poppy!" Then gasping with awareness of my blunder, I smiled ruefully, as she chuckled softly and assured me that she knew what I meant.

A bit later, I told her, "I guess we are just fated not to have a husband or a father."

"So it seems," she sighed. "I always worried about the winter driving and slippery roads.... We just have to be grateful that Poppy never knew what happened and did not feel any pain."

In a letter to her sister, Doré described what she did next, "It was hard to comfort Judy, so I told her that I had work for her to do. I said that if she and I felt as awful as we did about Poppy going on to far adventures without his girls, she must imagine how much more difficult it must be for his mother, who gave him life and had loved him so much longer. So I asked her to take care of Mom Goss and cheer her up and help her in every way she could."

Dorothy later told Doré that her words had been inspired. "By following your advice," she said, "Judy had someplace to put her own sorrow while she considered Mom."

I did all I could to help prepare for the funeral to be held in the Skylodge living room, soon filled with folding chairs.

Although Doré raised me outside of any religion, I could see that the traditional Methodist ritual gave Mom Goss some peace. I remember the silvery casket in front of the fireplace, draped with a spring-like blanket of freesia, iris and mimosa. I was thankful that the lid was closed and I could remember the way I had seen Poppy last—grinning from the door of my bedroom as he blew me a kiss goodnight.

I firmly believe that, had Don lived to companion my mother when she recovered and the three of us had a home of our own, we would have fashioned a mellow family life.

5

Skylodge

LUCKILY, Don's widowed mother invited him to bring me to live in the house where he had grown up. This warm, generous gesture, which I came to see as typical of her, meant that I could continue at my familiar junior high school with lifetime friends.

Always encouraged by my mother to "be a good sport," I tried to live up to her expectations. She had said, "Don't make things harder for Don" And "Be glad you can stay in Ann Arbor."

So, I accepted the plan with gratitude and only minor misgivings. None of us knew how long Doré would have to stay at the san. I hoped that this move would be temporary, so I tried to look on the bright side. Little did I know that I was in for such a radical change that I would feel like an actress in someone else's drama.

The enormous family homestead, called "Skylodge" was what might be considered a *mansion*. Three miles outside the city limits, it stood above broad sloping lawns at one end of two hundred acres of fields and woods. At first it reminded me of Tara in "Gone With the Wind." The difference was that a long gravel driveway encircled the lawns, and the commonly used doorway was in the rear, under a "porte cochere." Beyond that covered entrance was a separate three-car garage with an attached laundry room, where a black woman came once a week to do the washing and ironing.

The house was home not only to Mrs. Goss, but to Don's unmarried sister Dorothy, who was about 34, and his 28-year-old bachelor brother Kelly.

Inside the house, the two-story entrance hall nearly equaled the square footage of my former apartment. An elegant grandfather clock stood sentry beside the bottom of a graceful curved staircase that rose majestically to the second floor. When I began to look around, it was with a kind of wonder. It felt to me like a hotel.

A wide archway opened from the hall onto a long living room, dominated by a gleaming black grand piano. Dorothy Goss was a concert pianist who partially supported herself by giving lessons there at home. Near the fireplace, formal groupings of traditional sofas and chairs looked as if people seldom sat there, which was true. Two long tables held silver-framed family photographs. One depicted the family patriarch, Arnold Goss, the founder of the Kelvinator Corporation. I learned that he had been so distraught by the failure of some investments that he had taken his own life to provide insurance proceeds for his wife and family. Even as a self-absorbed adolescent, I felt that they would have given up their luxuries to have him in their lives.

Off the living room, another archway led to the "library," lined on all four walls with floor-to-ceiling bookcases, and centered with plump, soft sofas backed by long tables holding fringe-shaded reading lamps. At one of the desks, Kelly sometimes worked on accounts for the family business—an adjacent dairy farm called "The Oaklands." It boasted that its cows were "just Jerseys"—beautiful fawn-colored animals with large, dark chocolate eyes.

Across the central hallway, with its deep pile patterned rug, was the inviting, light-filled dining room. The ample oval table stood under a crystal chandelier, and another fireplace was centered on the far wall. Beyond the dining room was a large screened-in porch, which I later learned was used for summer suppers.

Swinging doors from that porch and from the dining room opened into a long narrow "butler's pantry" that held several sets of Spode and Wedgewood dishes in glass-fronted cabinets. From there, another door led to the kitchen, with its floor-to-ceiling cupboards painted beige. Typical of the 1920's, when the house was built, it was a strictly utilitarian space, with no decorative touches. The only work surface was an enamel topped table in the center of the room. The refrigerators were built into the wall of another pantry, where a commercial-sized Kitchen-Aid mixer stood ready for the bread dough Mrs. Goss entrusted to it twice a week.

When I was shown upstairs into one of the five bedrooms, I began to understand how living there would change my life. All the matching furniture was painted a soft gray, accented by thin rosy pink lines along the moldings. In addition to the high headboard and footboard of a full-size bed, the room held bedside cabinets, a highboy chest of drawers, desk and chair, and a grown-up lady's dressing table with long triple mirrors and a cane-seated bench. Later, when I climbed up on that bed and reclined against a bank of feather pillows, I wondered if I'd somehow been switched at birth and was really meant to be a princess.

But I was not pampered in that home. I was expected to do my share of household chores, and I learned to take *teasing*.

From being an isolated only child of a single parent, always treated as a miniature adult, I was thrust into a completely alien family life. It was quite an adjustment to become part of a boisterous bickering household that, in today's parlance, could only be called *dysfunctional*.

Kelly, an overgrown kid, was merciless. When he tickled me 'til I wept, held me down on the floor for his two Dalmatian dogs to lick, or made up "middle names" to kid me about losing my mittens or being chubby, it was difficult to accept that dishing out painful belittlement was his way of being a pal.

From his sister Dorothy, my new maiden aunt, I learned proper table settings, skin care, behavior expected of a young lady—and how her parents had ruined her life. Meanwhile, my new stepfather extended his devotion to my mother by becoming a great dad to me.

Profiles of Dorothy and Don Goss can be found in separate chapters entitled "If Only..." and "Poppy."

Don's mother, the quiet, caring matriarch, could not have been kinder to me. Taking in a teenager certainly changed her life, but, in a way, I served as something of a buffer. Kelly teased her, too, and Dorothy took out her own frustrations in bitchy criticism of her mom. I think that my loving appreciation of everything their gentle mother did cushioned those blows. I soon followed the example of her adult children and started calling her "Mom." It did not seem unnatural, because I called my own mother by her nickname, Doré.

As I ate my oatmeal at the kitchen table or dried the dinner dishes she washed, I loved hearing about Mom's girlhood on a farm in Lapeer—and how "Mister Goss" courted her as he drove with the top down on his roadster.

Looking back, I marvel at the inefficiency of the Skylodge kitchen. It was clearly designed for an era with household servants. But a change in the family fortune did not foster a change in design. All the dishes still had to be carried far across from the sink to be put away in the "butler's pantry." Flour and sugar for baking were stored in heavy, deep drawers.

In another lower drawer, two more large tins were almost always filled with cookies—the "hermits," a soft, spiced raisin cookie, and my favorite, chocolate chip. Mo always maintained that her cookies were perfectly healthy because they only contained "pure ingredients"—pure sugar, pure butter and pure chocolate!

Every day, she would pack two of these treats in my school lunch box, along with sandwiches made of leftover cold roast beef or peanut butter with sticky peach jam on homemade white bread. The rich, yeasty smell of that bread, as it baked, promised more than the product delivered. It was apparently beloved by her three adult children, but to me, the dense, dry, thin slices were about as appetizing as cardboard.

But, while I envied kids who got soft Wonder Bread, I knew I was lucky to have Mom's delicious sweet "chunk pickles."

Dinners were planned around predictable standards such as meat loaf, pork chops, beef roasts and fried chicken. I particularly loved her lamb stew. "Do" was a more creative cook—often concocting a seafood paella or chicken cacciatore, instructing me as she worked.

...

After Don's death, the Goss family allowed me to live on with them for another year. Doré paid for my food and clothing, but the responsibility for my upbringing was accepted by Mom Goss. I believe that her choice to care for me filled a void for her as well.

She sewed skirts for me from "good wool," because, she said, the ready made clothes in the stores were of such shoddy material. No grandchild of hers should be seen in them.

I tried to make myself useful to Mom when she entertained the Ann Arbor Garden Club, the Women's City Club, her PEO chapter or "Book and Thimble" Club.

Kelly willingly adapted his life to my needs by driving me three miles to the junior high school every weekday morning and picking me up again after work.

Dorothy had a number of artistic and intellectual friends who came for dinner occasionally. I felt proud and privileged when some guests made an effort to include me in conversations.

My school friends loved to visit me on weekends. Half-way along a dirt road between the house and the dairy farm was a huge barn full of hay, where we loved to play. After climbing the straight wooden ladder to the loft, we would lie back in the loose mounds to solve the problems of our adolescent lives. Other times, usually when my best friend David Hamberg came out, we would swing out on a long rope and jump from the loft into the piled hay below—then climb up to do it again.

The only telephone on the second floor of the house was on Mom's bedside table. She never minded if I sat on her bed for an hour or more in the evening while David and I figured out answers to our math homework, or even just talked about a movie.

Although separated from my mother for two critical adolescent years when she was hospitalized with Tuberculosis, I was lucky to live with the Gosses. The give and take of family life was a valuable experience for this only child.

Ten years later, Mom Goss offered to host my wedding reception at Skylodge, thus fulfilling a girlhood dream of tossing my bridal bouquet from the winding staircase. The reception line was centered on the living room fireplace— and the three-tiered cake held the place of honor amidst array of foods on the dining room table.

What special memories that mansion meant for me.

6

If Only

WHEN I MET my stepfather's sister, she was considered an old maid. Yet Dorothy Goss was only 35 when I appeared on her doorstep in 1941. She had no choice but to accept my presence. She still lived at home with her mother, who had agreed to take me in.

My own mother, Doré, had been diagnosed with seriously advanced tuberculosis and sent to a state TB sanatorium. Don Goss, her bridegroom of just three months was understandably reluctant to care for a 12-year-old step-daughter by himself. Luckily, he and I were invited to live with his family at Skylodge, their large five bedroom, four bath home on the outskirts of Ann Arbor.

Reared in privilege, Dorothy seemed to me to epitomize refined breeding and sophistication. Small in stature, perhaps only five feet two, she moved with a grace and poise that made her seem taller. Her platinum blonde hair was smoothed back from her face into a tightly wound bun at the nape of her neck.

A large silver-framed photograph of her on a living room side table revealed natural brown locks in earlier years.

Although not classically beautiful, the face she presented in public was artfully crafted, with eyebrows tweezed into thin dark lines, and pale thick powder layered onto a miniature nose and high cheekbones.

In clothing, Dorothy usually affected an English country manor style—such as a beige cashmere sweater set and a single strand of pearls above a tweed skirt, with silk stockings and sensible shoes. Some evenings, when she went out to concerts or plays with friends, she wore emeralds at the throat of a soft gray crepe dress. But, even in the summer, I never saw Dorothy in anything like the bright two-piece slacks suits or canvas slip-on shoes that my mother enjoyed.

Yet behind all the dignity and artifice with which Dorothy presented herself, there seethed an inner torment that she hugged to her bosom and nurtured as one might a deformed child. For many years, she had dwelled on what she saw as an injustice that had ruined her life. If only certain long ago events hadn't happened, she could have known happiness.

If only....

Dorothy felt trapped living at home, although the enormous white house could appropriately be called a mansion. She was accustomed to the luxuries of this elegant place, but it was, to her, a gilded cage.

An accomplished pianist, she thought of herself as a concert artist, but she made her living teaching. A succession of keyboard students, both children and adults, came to sit at the gleaming black grand piano in the living room.

Once a year or so, Dorothy would give a solo recital in an ornate small auditorium on the university campus. I loved listening to her practice as I did my homework upstairs, savoring the names of Chopin and Scriabin on my tongue along with their music in my ears. The excitement would build for weeks before the evening performance. I was allowed to hand out programs at the door, and when Dorothy came on the stage in a stunning wine velvet gown, I basked in the glamour of it all.

Even those critical successes couldn't fill the void for her. I didn't know why, but I could see that bitterness still shaped her days, and nothing eased the inner ache. Not the nightly martinis. Not the endless chain of cigarettes. And certainly not the tender attentions of her widowed mother, at whom she misdirected her rage. No question about it, Dorothy could be a real bitch. "Mother! You have no imagination!" she would rail. "Can't you think of anything besides meatloaf? This asparagus is tough. You overcooked it again. I've invited the Matthews for luncheon on Saturday. I think we should have a seafood salad. And please do remember to change into a nice dress. I can't bear it if you wear that gravy-stained apron."

Giving piano lessons could not have been Dorothy's goal. But it was necessary because of a reversal of fortune the family suffered a few years before I knew her. Some foolish investments caused her father to lose all his money. The family still had Skylodge only because he chose to take his own life to spare his wife and children an ignominious reduction in circumstance. As I gradually learned the story, I felt sure that they would have forsaken every penny of insurance money to have the patriarch alive. But he had gone out into the woods with a gun before any of them understood what was happening.

It was years before I learned everything behind the family dysfunction. At 12, I felt as if the world had just discovered that I was a long lost princess. No childhood dreams had ever foreshadowed my living in such a stately residence— dining every night at an enormous mahogany table set with linens, sterling silver, fine china and crystal—or writing my school assignments at an adorable small desk that matched all the other furniture in my sunny corner bedroom.

During the two years I lived at Skylodge, my new step-grandmother Gertrude Goss, nourished and clothed my body with savory meals, chocolate chip cookies and handmade woolen skirts. Dorothy took on the task of shaping my character. Although it distressed me to hear her irritable sniping at her mother, I was her willing acolyte.

My daily duties were table setting and dish drying. Toweling plates and glasses was no problem. I knew how to be careful, and I loved the time spent chatting with Grandma after dinner. But, before a meal, the ritual placement of several silver forks plus dessert spoons, soupspoons and teaspoons was a bit daunting. My mother had usually just handed me chopsticks with my bowl.

Dorothy was a patient instructor. She also assumed the role of intimate advisor on a number of subjects that might be grouped under the heading of "personal hygiene."

"Here, I bought you a complexion brush," she said one afternoon. "A clear skin is one of a girl's most valuable assets, and you are at the age when you may develop blackheads next to your nose."

Every night, she said, I must lather the little round brush on the imported facial soap she shared with me.

Then I was to work the brush in circles all over my forehead, chin and those pesky nostrils. After a thorough rinse came an astringent lotion to close the pores, followed by medicated face cream to combat dryness and leave my skin feeling soft.

Dorothy's recommended routines became second nature to me. Years later, I could hear her voice inside my head when I passed on her wisdom to my adolescent daughters.

A highlight of my day would be the after-school time spent in Dorothy's room, where exotic shiny black wallpaper was strewn with pastel flowers. Plopped shoeless on her peach satin comforter, I tried to absorb every grooming tip she described, eagerly waiting for her to drift off into reminiscences of her youth.

"They called us flappers in the twenties," she recalled, blowing cigarette smoke out over her upper lip as she gazed at her reflection above the silver-backed brushes on her dressing table. How I loved her tales of country club dances with dozens of beaus competing to bring her a cup of champagne punch.

Several of her girlhood summers included family trips abroad. One of the little tips for gracious living that she taught me was how to wash and press handkerchiefs while traveling.

"You can use shampoo or hand soap either one," she instructed me. "After rinsing and wringing out excess moisture, you carefully smooth the fabric onto the mirror in your hotel room. Take care to stretch the corners neatly and make sure that the entire surface adheres to the glass. When dry, *voila!* The square will look as if it was ironed by a laundress."

When she graduated from college, Dorothy spent three months in Europe alone! Well, not alone exactly—she traveled with two chums, but without parents and siblings. In Italy, she fell madly in love.

"Oh Judy! He was not only tall and handsome, with smooth black hair, he was a count—a distant member of the royal lineage," she proudly recalled.

As memories surfaced, she told me how the two of them met in Venice, when they fell into conversation between adjacent outdoor tables on the Piazza San Marco. She was impressed by his command of English, and he praised her halting phrases in Italian. Within a few days, she began slipping away from the other girls to join him as often as possible. Probably her friends were similarly occupied.

Dreamily, she told me of romantic gondola rides on moonlit Venetian canals with operatic arias floating on air.

"Never in his life had Luigi met anyone like me," she said. "He told me I was the most adorable girl he'd ever known." And never had Dorothy imagined being swept completely off her feet by a dashing young Italian nobleman.

As the final days of her summer sojourn drew near, the count was unwilling to give her up.

"He begged me to stay on and to marry him!" she told me. "I was so in love and I just knew that we would live happily ever after. So I cabled my parents that I would not be returning home and that they should start making plans to come to Venice for a wedding."

Listening, I started to wonder whether this would turn out well, and I couldn't wait to hear what happened next.

Her father came to Venice, all right! He came to accuse this so-called count of being a heartless, lying fortune hunter who knew a vulnerable American heiress when he saw one and who was motivated by greed, not love!

I can imagine the ensuing scene: irate father roaring at the scheming foreigner; injured Italian haughtily yelling in return; distraught daughter pleading tearfully with both men to trust her to know what she wants...

What Dorothy wanted carried no weight with Papa, who shoved her would-be husband out the front door of her hotel and forced her to promise she would never see him again.

"I was in shock," Dorothy said, painfully remembering that day. "Papa ordered me to pack my bags immediately, and of course I obeyed. But inside I was just furious, and I was crying so hard I could barely see what I was doing."

The next morning her father bundled her out to a waiting launch, hustled her onto a train and eventually a ship—where their long ocean voyage would give her plenty of time to consider the error of her ways.

What she considered first was jumping overboard. Later, she considered defying Papa and fleeing back to the arms of her lover. But she did neither. She dutifully acquiesced to her father's demands, and lived out the rest of her days in petulant resentment.

"I never forgave him," she told me. "I have always believed in my heart that if only I could have married Luigi, we would have been the happiest of couples."

If only...

No one in the family ever learned whether Luigi

Montefiore was really of the Italian nobility or was the scheming scoundrel that her father assumed him to be. The putative count never attempted to contact Dorothy in the States. Perhaps Papa had paid him off. Whatever the truth, Dorothy probably didn't want to hear it.

Clinging to the grief of being parted from the man she felt destined to marry, she refused to think about whether her lover was "good enough" for her or not. "I know he was as heartbroken as I was," she told me.

So rather than treasure the memories of those few weeks of joy, she cemented them behind a thick wall of anger that prevented her from ever loving again. No other suitor could measure up. Most soon ceased to try. Dorothy went through the motions of having a productive life, but she stayed trapped in misery.

For me, her story helped to explain her prickly personality. Even as an adolescent, I could understand that she had *chosen* to stay stuck in blame. She was contaminating her present by dwelling on regrets about the past. Her gilded cage was of her own making, so she never acknowledged that she could have flown.

If only...

After my mother's release from the hospital I returned to live with her in our own apartment. But we were always included in holiday celebrations at Skylodge, and, some years later, the family offered to host my wedding reception there. Dorothy helped to serve hors d'oeuvres and punch from that long mahogany dinner table, as guests marveled at the mansion, just as I had as a girl. At the end of that perfect afternoon, I tossed my bridal bouquet from the gracious curving staircase.

...

When Dorothy was diagnosed with cancer at the age of 60, she succumbed very quickly. No doctor suggested that her disease was of a particularly aggressive strain. But those who knew and loved her were not surprised that she failed to put up much of a fight. Most of life had been a bitter disappointment for her. Death may have seemed a welcome release.

Someone who believes in a hereafter where lovers are reunited might envision Dorothy running across a tiled piazza into the arms of her Italian count. I choose to honor her memory, and the vital role she played in my youth, by trying to live my own life without dwelling on

"Why me?"

"What if?" or

"If only."

馬

BOOK THREE

SCHOOL DAYS DISRUPTED

"Endurance can be a bitter root in one's life, bearing poisonous fruit, destroying other lives. Endurance is only the beginning. There must be acceptance, and the knowledge that sorrow fully accepted brings its own gifts. For there is an alchemy in sorrow. It can be transmuted into wisdom."

– Pearl Buck

1

Birdie and the Football Heroes

SCARCELY FIVE FEET TALL and weighing maybe 90 lbs, the white-haired ward helper banged open the door to our hospital room every day at 7 a.m.

"Good Morning Miss March. Good Morning Miss Reynolds," she would exclaim as she scurried over to raise clattering window blinds and let in the morning light. "How are we today?"

Her nickname on the medical TB floor of the University of Michigan Hospital was "Birdie"—doubtless inspired by the way this miniature person flitted around on her duties. Although the tubercular patients in her assigned rooms might wish they could turn over and go back to sleep, Birdie cheerfully thrust a bedpan at each of us and dashed off to clang metal basins in the sink as she filled them with water for washing. We braced for more clanging when she emptied them and stashed them on her rolling cart. Any momentary annoyance of ours was quickly overcome by Birdie's unfailingly lighthearted spirit.

I was fifteen. Ever since my mother, Doré, had been hospitalized for two years with a life-threatening case of Tuberculosis, I was given routine annual check-ups. The spring of my sophomore year in high school a chest x-ray showed a small lesion on my right lung.

Our family doctor, Marianna Smalley, explained, "TB is not caused by germs or a virus. It comes from something called a bacillus. A person becomes infected with the TB bacilli by close daily contact with someone who has the disease—a family member or co-worker. For you, it would have been back when Doré was sick, but not yet diagnosed..."

Seeing my confusion, Marianna hurried on, "Even when people are infected with tuberculosis, only about ten percent of them develop the disease. The other 90 percent never get sick. I hate having to tell you, Judy, but you are one of the unlucky ones."

I was lucky in one way: I had what was called a "minimal" case—not the "active" form. I had no cough, fever, or acute fatigue, and I was not contagious.

At first, Marianna thought that she could schedule me for medical procedures that would enable me to stay in school. In "pneumothorax" treatments, air is inserted through a long needle between a patient's ribs into the chest outside the lung. Pressure of this air collapses the lung, eventually arresting the TB lesion.

Medical specialists overruled her.

"We feel that only a regimen of complete bed rest can be counted on in Judy's case—to make sure it doesn't spread and get worse," a leading doctor declared.

I was ordered to drop all my sophomore classes without knowing when I would be able to return to high school. As devastating as this sentence was, I can't say it was unbelievable. Only a year had passed since my mother had been released from the hospital, so I remembered well what "bed rest" meant for someone with TB.

In one thing, Dr. Smalley did prevail.

"*Please* tell me that Judy won't be sent to Howell," Doré had begged. "I can't bear the thought of her being stuck in that old hell hole, with such lousy care and so far away."

In response to her dear friend's pleas, Marianna pulled every string she could, to arrange a bed for me in University Hospital instead of the state TB sanatorium thirty miles west. Even that isolation might have been preferable to the treatment in the late 19th or early 20th centuries. Then, doctors believed that fresh air alone could improve health, so patients were housed on cold sleeping porches or tents on roofs.

In the 1940s, the entire 7th floor of University Hospital was devoted to treatment of tuberculosis. The 8th floor housed those recovering from the drastic surgeries performed for TB back then. Doré had been a patient on both floors. She had endured her slow recovery with remarkable courage and good humor. So, much as I hated the whole idea of missing school and interrupting my life, I knew I had to make Doré proud by being the good sport she had raised me to be.

My gratitude for being able to stay in Ann Arbor matched my mother's. Knowing that she and my friends could easily visit me made my fate more acceptable.

Hospital days are so full of bustling activity that they do not drag as much as one might imagine. I passed some of the uninterrupted time by writing letters on a clipboard braced against bent knees, reading, pasting school pictures in a scrap book, listening to pop music and football games on a small radio in an ivory plastic case, and talking with my room mate.

Jean Reynolds, also 15, had been a classmate of mine all through school, so we had a basis for deepened friendship. It was a lucky break for both of us that we were bunked in together and didn't suffer loneliness. Indulgent nurses had managed to find each of us an extra bedside stand. So the business-like items such as water pitchers and basins could be on one side of our beds and our personal radios, books and pictures on the dry surface of the other stand.

We were allowed to sit up against a few pillows for the ablution routine and for the breakfast on trays that followed. Then our treatment required lying flat on our backs until lunchtime. Afternoons started with an hour-long nap before time stretched out until we heard the rattle of the supper tray carts.

Hospital meals are never gourmet fare, but I enjoyed certain foods that were novelties to me, such as a salad of shredded carrots and raisins with French dressing. Peas were sometimes served with peanuts, and at other times with cubes of yellow cheese. A half banana on a bed of lettuce would be covered with mayonnaise and crushed peanuts. Our mothers kept us supplied with treats and a stash of seasonings to liven up the hospital food.

Jean was allowed to have her tabletop phonograph. Piano concertos were among her favorite records and new to me.

"Haven't you even heard these by Tchaikovsky and Rachmaninoff?!" she asked.

"No. We've never listened to this kind of music at home. Doré likes jazz and show tunes."

One day I said, "That's pretty. What is it?"

"It's the morning theme from Grieg's *Pier Gynt Suite*," she told me. I remain grateful for Jean's gentle tutelage as I developed an appreciation for classical music.

In 1944, television was still a luxurious novelty, unheard of in ordinary homes and certainly not a part of the furnishings as it is in today's hospital rooms. Maybe that was a blessing. With soap operas or game shows to fill my days, I might never have read such weighty classics as *Vanity Fair*.

Reading heavy books is something of a challenge while lying on your back. Fortunately, some former patient devised a solution. Ingenious book racks were attached to metal rods that swung around over each bed. Above our heads, as we lay flat, a book could be positioned on a wooden panel and held in place by metal clamps against the front and back hard covers. Pages were secured by lightweight wire clips. To turn a page, I needed only to raise one hand long enough to lift the tiny place holder.

In addition to bed rest, certain medical procedures were used to help rest the lung. In my case, the doctors prescribed the very pneumothorax treatments that Dr. Marianna Smalley had hoped could keep me out of the hospital.

Using a very long, thick needle, thrust through my side between the ribs, a doctor pumped air into the space between my chest wall and my lung. It was a good thing I was lying on my side, prepped with local anesthetic, so I wasn't frightened by the sight of that instrument of potential torture. I later learned that, as air filled the space, it pushed against my lung, collapsing it. The "pneumos," as they were called, were given daily at first, then weekly as long as the lung learned to stay in its new resting position. The procedure was not as painful as it might sound. Eventually, I learned to take the needle between my ribs without a local anesthetic. Believe it or not, the sting of that preliminary injection was worse than the pressure of the larger air needle.

The most popular patients on 7th Floor that year were two celebrated University of Michigan football players. For much of the public, the news of their illness blew the image of a tubercular patient as an emaciated wraith. When a male classmate of ours from high school was hospitalized and assigned to the athletes' four-bed room, Jean and I got to meet those heroes. As our girlfriends outside learned that we knew Tom Kuzma and Julius Franks, we had plenty of visitors. "Julie" Franks and I remained friends for many years.

As patients beginning treatment, though, none of us laid eyes on each other except on the long-anticipated entertainment nights. Once a month, staff rolled all of our beds out to a vast solarium and lined them up in rows to hear live music or watch old movies projected on a large screen. Everyone looked forward to those nights as much as lonely soldiers on an island outpost might anticipate the arrival of a USO troupe.

We girls fussed over what bed jackets to wear with as much excitement as debutantes comparing ball gowns.

"Are you going to wear those new flowered pink pajamas Doré brought you," Jean asked me.

"Yes, I think so. Do you have an extra hair ribbon that would go with them?"

Lipstick, rouge and cologne helped us feel as if we were about to have a date, instead of lying six feet apart from a boy in another metal hospital bed.

"I hope Doctor Jenkins is there tonight," I told Miss Almond.

"Oh, I'm pretty sure he will be," she answered, chuckling. The head nurse knew that most of the female patients, and probably staff members too, had a crush on Dan Jenkins, the handsome, curly-haired resident from Texas.

As patients got to know each other, many, especially the teenagers and college students, found ways to communicate, share information and relieve feelings of isolation.

Accommodating nurses could be counted on to pass notes or books or magazines back and forth between rooms. Patients even played games such as "Battleship" by writing their moves on bits of paper slipped into a uniform pocket.

"You sank my aircraft carrier and got one other hit," the note would say. "Now give me A4, B3 and C2." It might be hours before Miss Martin or Mrs. Cofer would remember to deliver that vital communiqué, so the games could go on for days.

In the fall of 1944, Jean and I were moved to a four-bed ward with two new roommates. Rita Travers, 14, who came from a nearby farming community, was dark-haired and shy. We three teen-agers exchanged movie magazines and talked the nurses into pinning a five foot high photo poster of Frank Sinatra on the frame of a cloth screen that was wheeled across the open door as needed for privacy.

Our fourth roommate, Harriet DeSoto, 25, was both den mother and model *femme fatale.* She regaled her delighted young audience with tales of wild undergraduate days and her eventual marriage to a doctor much older than herself.

She may have embellished the stories for our amusement, but we certainly gained a colorful education that went far beyond the basic facts of life.

My most endearing memory of Harriet is of her miming jitterbug dancing with her hands alone, while lying flat in bed with her elbows tight to her sides. As the radio provided band music, she twirled her fingers and swished her hands, remembering what her whole body could once do with a partner on a dance floor.

One unpleasant memory of that room is of the time when a young intern led the weekly medical "rounds."

I was accustomed to seeing a troupe of doctors arrange themselves around the foot of my bed, peering down and smiling beneficently as they asked, "And how are you feeling today, Miss March?"

Then, as I lay there with a small hand towel covering my breasts, they would take turns placing their stethoscopes on my chest and mumbling knowingly about whatever they were supposed to be hearing—or not.

On the Friday in question, the particularly smarmy intern asked, "Do you mind if we move this?" meaning the towel. Thinking that he simply wanted to shift the fabric to get a better listen, I nodded. This was routinely done without asking a patient's permission.

Striving to remain a straight-faced professional, he *whipped* the towel aside! The other interns gasped in surprise as my fifteen-year-old bosom was completely exposed. So did Jean as, from the next bed, she witnessed the unprecedented transgression. Shock kept me from gasping in embarrassment, but I can guess that my face was red.

The playboy, who clearly thought he had been terribly clever, grinned as he tossed the towel back at me and sauntered out of the room, followed by shamefaced colleagues, one of whom had the grace to mutter, "Sorry."

It was probably wise, even compassionate, that doctors didn't initially tell patients that they might have to be hospitalized for a year or more. Each month they checked the level of bacilli in my phlegm, called sputum, and I was taken on a rolling gurney for a new chest x-ray. Then, Dr Jenkins, accompanied by a covey of interns, would stand at the foot of my bed and make a strained attempt to be both grave and upbeat in his pronouncements.

"Things look good," he would maintain. "The lesion is beginning to calcify. We'll take another look next month and see."

When I was allowed to sit up in bed part of the day, I took advantage of crafts offered by occupational therapists. Not only did I learn to tool and lace leather billfolds and notebook covers, I etched designs on copper and aluminum coasters, trays and glass tumblers. It was fun to have secrets from Doré and other family members that Christmas.

The hospital staff did all they could to make the holidays festive with bright decorations and special mealtime treats. Jean's mother and mine strung colored lights on a small fir tree in our room, and friends in our high school choir came up to sing carols for us and the other patients.

And so the days and weeks stretched into six long months before I heard the magic words: "You can start dangling."

2

Dangling

"JUDY CAN START dangling tomorrow!"

As my exciting news was passed from room to room along the University Hospital corridor, all the other tuberculosis patients rejoiced. They knew that it meant the beginning of the end for one fellow "lunger" after her long stay on the Medical TB floor.

It meant that after six months of complete bed rest, flat on my back except for meals, I was about to begin the slow process of preparing to get up, and eventually to get out.

Each morning, I could sit up and dangle my legs over the side of the bed for five minutes. The following week, I could dangle for five minutes in the morning and five minutes in the afternoon. In another week, the time was increased to ten minutes in the morning and then ten minutes twice a day.

This frustratingly slow procedure was required, the doctors assured me, to accustom my weakened, wasted limbs to the flow of blood to their muscles. It was astonishing to see how much my muscles had atrophied in six months. The calves of my pale legs waved like banners in a breeze. It was understandable that such loose, flabby muscles could complain if asked to support body weight too soon.

Finally, about a month after all the initial excitement, I was helped off the bed into a chair. Those next five minutes, feeling the floor under slippered feet before being assisted back between the sheets, made the end seem real. Out of bed! What a thrill!

In the months that followed, my "up time" in the chair was extended in five-minute increments to half an hour both morning and afternoon. And then, finally, good news would travel along the corridor again:

"Judy is walking!"

No year-old toddler taking her first steps could be showered with more enthusiastic encouragement than a long-hospitalized patient who can finally move outside the four walls of her room. Without question, the greatest pleasure was being able to give up using bedpans! The bathroom across the hall was my first destination.

Perhaps only a prisoner released from a jail cell can appreciate the joy of being able to shuffle along the hallway into a neighboring ward to visit other, still bedridden, patients, who had become friends.

In another three months, I put on real clothes and shoes, bid my friends goodbye and accepted their applause as I walked out. Although I had done my best to keep my spirits high, eleven months in the hospital had taken a big chunk out of my young life.

Even at home that spring, my up time was limited. I still

spent half of each day propped against bed pillows, and I continued to receive weekly pneumothorax treatments. But I'll never forget the thrill of walking on grass, breathing the sweet fragrance of blossoming lilacs, and relishing the yellow brightness of daffodils.

Although I had hated algebra in ninth grade, I found geometry intriguing that summer. And I made an unexpected friend. Ruth was 20, the wife of a worker at Willow Run defense plant. She decided to use her time to pursue a postponed high school diploma. Often, after class, she would walk home with me to huddle over homework. It boosted my confidence to be the math tutor, and she added to my education about the life of an older woman. When she and Dave went home to Newport News, Virginia, letters kept us connected for several years. A tiny black-and-white snapshot of Ruth with their infant daughter is still vivid in my mind.

Our longed-for month of August in Pentwater was made possible because I was able to continue my "pneumo" treatments up north. By a lucky coincidence, a friend of ours in the village was a doctor who had also been hospitalized with TB. Jack Heysett had even learned to insert the needle through his own ribs to deliver the air into his chest cavity to temporarily collapse his lung! Now, with his disease arrested, he was working at the hospital in the neighboring town of Hart and arranged to treat me there.

I still wonder if Doré wished I had read more literature that summer instead of movie magazines. I can't recall her suggesting it, although she didn't always say what she thought. But I remain grateful that she did not raise an eyebrow when asked to admire the bulging scrapbooks I filled with clippings about Lana Turner and my heartthrob, Alan Ladd.

When we returned to Ann Arbor in September, I was permitted to go back to high school full time, but I still had to arrange to take all my classes in the morning and study in bed in the afternoon. A few friends could study at home with me, if their parents understood I was not infectious, but most days I loathed my isolation.

No extra-curricular clubs or choirs were allowed either, so I concentrated on academics. Scholastic honors and achievements won me adult approval. But as a "brain," who couldn't go dancing or skating, I just pressed my face against an invisible pane separating me from so-called normal teen-aged fun.

Yet, over the next two summers, Pentwater worked its special magic. New friends there didn't know I was smart, so I had lots of dates and even a couple of intense youthful romances.

By late spring of my senior year, the doctors released their grip enough to allow me to go on the class trip to Washington, DC and New York City. None of my classmates could possibly have been more excited than I was. Heedless of my reduced lung capacity, I climbed to the top of the Washington Monument.

In Manhattan, between rushing to see the Statue of Liberty and Grant's Tomb, I managed one free afternoon to spend with my beloved aunt, Lurry. Joyfully we shopped at the legendary Lord and Taylor's and had a dinner of authentic Chinese food cooked by her friend Pearl Chan. With my fellow students, I saw the Broadway hits "Born Yesterday" starring Judy Holladay and the new Rogers and Hammerstein musical "Carousel" with John Raitt.

By the time I heard "Pomp and Circumstance" at the Ann Arbor High School graduation and walked across the stage at Hill Auditorium, just one year behind my original class, I felt normal again.

My summer suitor Art Westlund wanted to set a wedding date. He even built an impressive log cabin on the shores of Silver Lake, to lure me into a commitment. But I had been accepted at Oberlin, and his dreams of domesticity were no match for my own of—COLLEGE!

3

Frank Sinatra and the Pants Pressers

JUNE OF 1945 was one of the few times that my mother did not head her blue Ford north the day after the University semester ended.

Doré expected to spend the whole summer in the village of Pentwater on the shores of Lake Michigan. Our old house there, which she had remodeled and colorfully decorated, had been her beloved refuge since I was two years old.

But that year, I begged to stay in Ann Arbor for the first six weeks of vacation, because my doctors had allowed me to go to summer school.

I knew that Doré would have a conniption at the thought of staying in our apartment. In a commercial block, it was a dark, cramped space above a dry-cleaning store. It was all we could find in 1943, when she was released from her own hospitalization for TB.

With the United States at war against Adolph Hilter and his Axis cronies in Europe, workers from the nation's southern states had swarmed north to earn big bucks making bombers at the Willow Run defense plant. Even the academic sanctuary of nearby Ann Arbor overflowed with new families who snapped up every available rental. Doré and I couldn't have picked a worse time to relocate. But we didn't exactly pick it. It just had to be.

With the help of friends, we carried belongings up the 42 steps to a tiny apartment that opened onto a dark hall above the dry cleaners. The door from the central hall opened onto another dark hallway. Inside, this narrow passage led past a bathroom and the galley—which was too small to be called a kitchen—to the living room where light, at last, could be seen coming in the two windows overlooking a busy street. A curtained archway separated the living room from the alcove that allowed enough space for my single bed and dresser. It boasted the only other window that let in light. Doré moved her own bed into what was intended to be a dining space, between the living room and the galley. The window revealed only the brick wall of another commercial building next door.

Home Sweet Home. We had moved in September, in time for me to start high school and Doré to return to her job on the university campus. At least the location, on East Williams, a block off State Street, was within convenient walking distance of both destinations. And once we had some of our own furniture delivered from storage and some familiar pictures hung on the walls, the place was livable. So what if I could never host a big party the way other kids did? My life alone with a widowed mother was so unlike the pattern in other kids' homes that I didn't care.

During the winter, I hadn't been particularly aware of

the dry cleaners. I had to pass it, of course, before lugging grocery bags up that long flight of stairs to the apartment. But it was just there. "A fact of life," as Doré would say. But, with no air conditioning in those days, and not even any cross-ventilation, it was bound to be extremely uncomfortable in the summer.

"Oh, Judy," Doré said. "I can't bear the thought of living in this hot, stuffy apartment all of July! It will be unbearable."

"But if I can take two classes this summer," I pleaded, "I can start making up some of the school I missed."

I would have to take both classes in the mornings, come home at noon and study in bed. But it would be worth it. I knew that the time I had spent in the hospital would still put me one year behind my original high school class, so making up the extra half year mattered to me.

"I don't want to graduate another semester later, in the middle of the year," I told my mother. "It would mean waiting even longer before starting college."

"Yes, of course. I can see that.... I do understand," she said, resignedly. "And much as I hate to postpone feeling the blessed 'coolth' of Pentwater, I don't want you to have to stay here alone."

"Oh thank you," I exclaimed. "At least we can look forward to the whole month of August under the shade of 'three maples and an oak.'" That was Doré's way of describing the front of our lot. "Maybe I'll even be able to go to the beach by then," I said.

July over the Perfect Touch Dry Cleaning store was even worse than expected. It made sense that the employees of the business below worked at night, when it was cooler for them.

But in our apartment above, with muggy weather dictating open windows, our sleep was usually long delayed.

As if the Whump! Hisssssssss! Klang! and the acrid odor of cleaning fluid and damp hot fabric weren't enough to create discomfort, there was the radio. The radio downstairs had to be played loudly enough to be heard by the workers above their machines. Far into the night, the pressing machines protested loudly as they endured forced labor to produce flat, creased pants to the voice of Frank Sinatra:

"Alone from night to night you'll find me,
too weak to break the chains that bind me,"
"I need no shackles to remind me,
I'm just a prisoner of love."

Prisoner chained by a fiery furnace, I imagined, as I lay stretched out in baby doll pajamas doing homework. At least I got to hear the Hit Parade.

One evening, as Doré sat reading in the living room, she was puzzled enough to stick her head around the corner into my bed alcove to ask, "Why is that man singing about the President?"

"Huh?" I said. "What're you talking about?"

"That singer," she said, "on the radio downstairs. He's singing something about the President and the moon."

Mystified, I paid more attention to the strains of a popular song wafting up with the pungent fumes from below. As I listened closely I identified Sinatra singing "Full Moon and Empty Arms," the plaintive love song based on a melody from Rachmaninoff's *Second Piano Concerto*.

"Full Moon and Empty Arms
The moon is there for us to share
But where are you?"

"There! Did you hear it?" Doré asked. "Listen! It doesn't make any sense. Why is he singing 'Full moon and FDR'?"

With President Franklin D. Roosevelt being mentioned so often on the radio toward the end of World War II, we were all accustomed to hearing reporters refer to him by his initials FDR.

That hot summer night, I realized with amusement that Doré thought she heard "FDR" when Sinatra sang of "empty arms." After I explained the music's lonely complaint, we shared a good laugh.

The memory of that night—with its oppressive heat, the open windows, the pop music blaring over the racket of steam presses and illogical lyrics—brought a tender smile to my lips long after we shook off the discomforts of two summers above the dry cleaners.

4

The Jolson Story

BACK IN THE 1940'S, when I was in high school, movie theaters showed the pictures continuously. If you bought a ticket for the one o'clock show, you could just remain in your seat for the three o'clock showing and on through for the 5:00, 7:00 and 9:00. No one cared, and no usher ever asked you to leave.

This was not my usual behavior, but in one memorable month, Marilyn Dressel and I took advantage of that *laissez faire* attitude. We watched "The Jolson Story" fifteen times!

First, some background. Marilyn sat behind me in homeroom when she was a sophomore and I had returned to the 11th grade after a year in a TB ward. A diminutive red head, she was as cute and perky as I was tall and chunky. It's hard to say why we hit it off. Our home life was quite different, too. She and her big brother Bob lived with two parents in a large house in a leafy residential neighborhood. I lived with my widowed mother in a dark, narrow apartment above a dry-cleaning shop.

We both wore saddle shoes and bobby sox, of course. And short plaid skirts topped by long sweaters. We both envied the girls who were swallowed up in their boyfriends' "letter sweaters"—cardigans adorned with 8 inch embroidered "AA" patches they earned for playing Ann Arbor High sports.

"What do you think Bud sees in Annabelle?" I might ask Marilyn. "I dunno," she'd answer. "Maybe she lets him cop a feel." In our innocence, neither of us would have suspected that they *went all the way.*

"Did you understand what Miss Tinkham was talking about in World History," Marilyn asked me.

"Not exactly," I said. "But if The Great War was supposed to end all wars, it sure didn't work."

We cemented our bond by spending many after-school hours grilling each other on French verb endings. Years later I learned that Miss Anna Steele did her language students no favors by not insisting on proper pronunciation, but more than 60 years later, Marilyn and I could still recite, in unison, the five sentences that we all committed to memory the first week of that class.

"J'entre dans la salle de classe.
Je regarde autour de moi.
Je vois les éleves et le professeur.
Je dit 'Bonjour' au professeur.
Je prends ma place."

The two of us had something else in common: we both spent our summers "up north." Unlike classmates who stayed in hot, humid Ann Arbor or were crammed in a family car for long driving trips, Marilyn and I spent from mid June to early September in resort towns.

Marilyn's family rented a house trailer in a state park in Beulah, on Crystal Lake, in Benzie County. My mother and I loved our big, old Pentwater village house near Lake Michigan in Oceana County. Not that we thought much about it then, but our summer living conditions were the reverse of how we each lived in the winter. Summers, we both earned spending money by waitressing. She wore a cute red-and-white uniform at The Cherry Hut, a tourist attraction featuring pies and jams made from Michigan's most celebrated tart fruit. In the Pentwater Dairy Bar, I made sandwiches and dished up ice cream sundaes behind the counter.

It was in the fall of 1946 that Marilyn and I fell utterly in love with "The Jolson Story." The biopic about the jazz age singer Al Jolson won an academy award for best picture that year. On *three* Saturdays, Marilyn and I smuggled hamburgers and milk shakes into Ann Arbor's State Theater. That, plus some popcorn and Milkduds, sustained us for the whole afternoon and evening of watching the movie over and over and over again.

We learned all the words to all the songs: "Toot, Toot, Tootsie Goodbye," "California Here I Come," and the iconic "Mammy." Most of the dialogue, too. I guess you could say that we were Larry Parks' groupies, although that expression was unknown back then. It was Al Jolson's own voice that Parks lip synced. So, Jolson was our real hero. Luckily, our parents indulged us in this teenaged obsession, and Mr. Dressel picked us up in front of the movie theater at 11:00 each night.

Over the years, Marilyn and I often fondly recalled that exploit. Other kids probably pulled that same stunt for other films, but we considered the memory our private delight.

100

During our child-rearing years, still living in Michigan, Marilyn and I managed to meet about four times a year. We would plot and scheme to spend one entire day alone together at a spot about equidistant from the cities where we lived. In the mid-state town of Cadillac, the Sun and Snow Resort offered us a comfortable lounge and an adjacent restaurant for lunch. There we poured out truths about our lives.

In Big Rapids, Marilyn was a floral designer, creating not only stunning wedding bouquets, but imaginative décor with artificial plants in her own home. An enormous willow tree drooped over the dining table, and palm fronds surrounded the shower. In Traverse City, I had become a reporter and section editor for the regional daily newspaper. We also compared notes on our growing kids—we each had four—and our marriages, supporting and encouraging each other through the rough spots. We occasionally brought our families together, too, either in Traverse City, Big Rapids, Beulah, or Pentwater. After I moved to New Jersey in 1980, we wrote letters and visited each other every few years.

In 1994, I found a VHS tape of *The Jolson Story.* When my second husband, Ethan Davis, and I visited Marilyn and her husband Bucky at their unique Big Rapids home, we gave her the video. Flooded with nostalgia, we told the men the story behind the presentation.

"Can you *believe* that?!" Bucky exclaimed; eyes wide with astonishment.

"Why would anyone want to see the same movie ten times?" Ethan rejoined.

"*Fifteen* times!" Marilyn corrected him.

"Probably because we were young and foolish," I told them. "But c'mon and watch the film with us..."

As the four of us viewed it together, the guys marveled at their wives' ability to recall so much of the action and Jolson's music. If they thought that we had been nuts, they kindly refrained from telling us. And the whole story increased their understanding of the strong bond between their wives.

For Marilyn and me, it was a delight to relive and share that memory of our youth.

5

Oberlin

ANN ARBOR IS not only my hometown; it is the home of one of the nation's finest universities. My father had been on Michigan's faculty when I was a small child and my mother on the staff as long as I could remember. At 18, I lived within easy walking distance of the campus. It might seem logical that I would choose to further my education there. It certainly would have saved money.

But, like most kids, I wanted to go away from home and live in a college dorm. And my mother was supportive of my wish to attend a small, liberal arts school. Through her job, Doré got to know many students who considered the University of Michigan an impersonal "diploma factory." That was not true of everyone, nor of every aspect of campus life, but the vast scale and maze of the school did allow some people to slide through barely noticed.

Oberlin College in Ohio was my first choice. In addition to its academic excellence, I admired its history as the first institution of higher learning in the country to admit African-Americans, and later the first to admit women. The absence of fraternities and sororities also appealed to me. Some Michigan co-eds I'd met told me about the humiliating hazing they had endured in their sororities and about the practice of "black balling" unacceptable applicants for their sisterhood—primarily girls of color.

Doré willingly endorsed Oberlin because of its outstanding History of Art Department. At that time, we both assumed that I would go into the family business and become a museum curator. When I had been admitted, she assured me that her savings could cover the tuition. My Grandfather March had carefully invested the proceeds of Ben's life insurance. This had always been earmarked for my college education, and she believed that he would approve of my plans.

My mother also assumed that the Oberlin Art Department would want to know that one of the incoming freshmen had a distinguished heritage. Doré's visit to campus over Thanksgiving weekend gave her the chance to tour the Allen Art Museum.

As a curator showed us the Asian collection, Doré said, "Mrs. King, I think you'll be interested to know that Judy's father was Benjamin March."

"Oh my," responded the white-haired scholar, "No wonder your name seemed familiar. I will never forget the time that Mr. March came here to help me set up my first exhibition of Chinese paintings." Smiling somewhat shyly, she recalled, "He was so charming and so willing to share his wealth of information. He treated me like a trusted colleague and gave me the confidence I needed to mount the show."

It didn't surprise my mother to know that Mrs. King had never forgotten him.

None of us could have imagined, in 1947, that my father's expertise in the field of Asian Art would still be applauded more than eighty-five years after his death. How I wish that Doré could have heard the words of Katy Ryor, the young art historian I met in China in 1993, and, later, the testimony of Smithsonian archivist David Hogge, who <u>still</u> hears the name of Benjamin March evoked at current scholarly conferences.

With apparent pleasure, Mrs. King added, "I am so glad you chose Oberlin, Judy, and I certainly hope you'll be happy here."

The college turned out to be a perfect choice for me. Suzie Burnett, from Youngstown, Ohio, was a compatible roommate. In physical stature, we were complete opposites, so we could never swap clothes. But we had both shopped for long, full skirts that reached almost to our ankles—required for "The New Look" in fashion that year. We had agreed, through letters, to advance purchase of matching bedspreads, and thought we were terribly clever when we hung a sign on the outside of our door naming our room as "Dew Drop Inn."

We soon easily agreed on how to structure our days. Suzie had less free time than I did, because she "sat bells" on the Gulde House switchboard to earn her room and board. My schedule had to include therapy to prevent a recurrence of TB. Dr. Smalley, our family physician who had monitored my recovery, insisted that I be protected by continuing pneumothorax treatments. Each week, by pre-arrangement, a friendly female taxi driver took me thirty miles to a private hospital, where I could get the injections of air in my chest cavity to keep my lung collapsed. This ample African-American woman always waited while I received my treatments, and we both enjoyed our conversations as she drove me back to my dorm.

The other girls in Gulde House were congenial. In addition to our late-night gab sessions and fashion consultations, we were all excited about the coming marriage of Great Britain's Princess Elizabeth to the dashing Phillip Mountbatten. I'll never forget huddling together over my small bedside radio to hear the scratchy international broadcast of the wedding ceremony and the recessional parade from Westminster Abbey to Buckingham Palace where the couple waved to the crowds. Without the visuals provided by television in later years, we were dependent back then on the words of skilled announcers to provide descriptions of the festive scene.

I made additional friends in the stimulating classes and campus activities. My favorite course at Oberlin was Mediaeval Architecture taught by Clarence Ward. Although he held a Ph.D. degree, he insisted on being called mister. "A doctor," he said, "is presumed to be a physician." In class, Mr. Ward entertained us with illustrated tales of climbing around on the flying buttresses of Chartres Cathedral in his "plus fours" knickers—back in the twenties.

His expertise in his field inspired me to create a large chart of architectural elements that I illustrated with sketches of Romanesque and Gothic columns, capitals, arches, vaults and ribs. After I left the college, that chart evoked such warm memories that I kept the yellowing, rolled relic until I moved to Las Fuentes retirement resort in 2011, when it finally "bit the dust," as Doré would have said. For the record, I also discarded a large scrapbook bulging with concert bulletins, news clippings, dance programs, dried corsages, report cards, drawings, notes, and other once-vital memorabilia. It's rather embarrassing to admit that I had lugged that around from home to home for *sixty-two* years!

Once a month, Mr. and Mrs. Ward would host a Sunday afternoon tea for students in their gracious, colonial Oberlin home. Between bites of sweet pastries, we politely disclosed the progress of our young lives and confided ambitions.

The name of their grandson, Geoffrey C. Ward, may be familiar to viewers of Ken Burns' Public Television series *The Civil War* and, more recently, *The Roosevelts*. A noted historian, Geoff Ward co-produced those and Burns' other popular documentaries.

Every four years, Oberlin College held a "Mock Convention" to choose its preferred candidate for President of the United States. Without any presumption that the Democrat or Republican Parties would pay attention to the result, political science majors, and many other students, received valuable, hands-on education from the event. As a freshman, I felt lucky to witness the excitement in the spring of 1948, and I paid more attention that summer when our chosen candidate, Harry Truman, won the Democratic nomination.

...

There was no dining room in my small dorm, which was a converted three-story house. We took our meals at May Cottage, a much larger residence hall across the street. There, early in my freshman year, I met Phillip Miller Allen. A brainy sophomore, Phil was a waiter on a work-study scholarship similar to Suzie's. He epitomized "tall, dark and handsome."

In fact, his height of 6-feet-2 made me, at 5'9," feel comfortably average. We shared a love of classical music and poetry and, throughout that school year, we studied together as often as our schedules would permit. I soon understood the meaning of "falling head over heels."

Phil was the first guy that I ever seriously considered marrying. At spring vacation, I went with him to spend the week at his house in Hamilton, Ohio. His widowed mother and sister Dorcas, a student nurse who still lived at home, offered me a warm welcome. With both of them gone during the day, Phil and I seized the rare opportunity of privacy to be naked together. Although we delighted in discovering and caressing each other's bodies, we did not allow ourselves to go "all the way." Very square by later standards, we were both conditioned to believe in saving intercourse for marriage.

When my mother visited the Oberlin campus during her own spring break, she approved our fledgling commitment to a future together. But, despite our admiration for each other and passionate love, Phil and I eventually acknowledged some critical differences in what we wanted out of life.

At the end of the summer, when he came to spend a week with me in Pentwater, Phil had no interest in swimming or lying on the beach, preferring to read at a picnic table. I was surprised, and somewhat disappointed, but let it go. We both enjoyed long walks around the village and down along the marina. But then, Saturday evening, he refused to go with me to the Oceana County Fair. He considered such frivolous activities a complete waste of time. I was unwilling to give up the baby animals, handicraft displays and carnival games and rides that I had looked forward to every year since childhood. So, I went ahead on my own, joining a group of friends. While I was gone, Phil confided in my mother over his torn feelings. She tried to explain that we thought that life was more than serious endeavor—that it should include some lighthearted fun. She told him that marriage to my father had required compromise between his devotion to scholarly pursuits and her desire to go dancing or see a stage play. Their willingness to find a balance between their separate interests ensured happiness for each of them. Fortunately, they both loved dinner parties and entertaining guests. Phil acknowledged that he felt no need for social groups.

Doré confessed that she had been concerned about my relationship with him when I'd written home from college my freshman year, full of excitement about having persuaded him to go to a movie. It worried her because that sort of date seemed perfectly natural to her. Phil easily recalled the evening, admitting that agreeing to waste time and money that way had been a major concession on his part. It had never happened again. He told Doré that he admired my intellectual curiosity. He knew that I loved learning. But he also knew I loved movies, and he was firm in his distaste for such activities. The idea of carnival rides appalled him. She later told me that she could see his heartache.

When I arrived home from the County Fair, he was waiting up. We sat propped against the headboard of my bed, holding each other as we talked until dawn. His bus was due to leave later that morning. We agreed that it was a good thing he visited my beloved summer home.

"I'm glad you came," I said. "It would never have occurred to me that what I love to do here would seem so shallow to you." I could feel him wince at that word, but he appreciated that I acknowledged his feelings. Kissing my forehead and tightening his arm around my shoulders, Phil sighed before responding, "I hate to sound holier-than-thou, but it's true that spending every afternoon at the beach and a whole evening at a carnival seem pointless to me."

Finally, with shared tears of disappointment, but no bitterness, we agreed to break up. We could see no future together. Reflecting on it now, I can't imagine ever having a family with him. How would he have wanted to raise children? I wish I could remember how he was parented. Was his father stern? Did he leave? Were he and Phil's mother divorced? I don't know. It doesn't matter now.

Back at Oberlin that fall, we caught sight of each other on campus now and then, but rarely crossed paths. Suzie had a talk with him once, later telling me that he was still carrying a torch. But he and I didn't speak again for some 60 years.

After I published a book about my mother, I wrote to tell Phil. We enjoyed catching up by correspondence until he died two years later.

...

Suzie and I drew the lowest number for a room assignment in our sophomore dormitory at Oberlin. Allencroft was another old, converted house that held a wide assortment of room sizes. Ours was so narrow only a bunk bed would fit. I was grateful that Suzie, at 5'1" and about 100 lbs, was willing and agile enough to scramble up the rickety wooden structure to sleep on top. At least we had separate small desks under two nice windows looking out over the front of the house.

I was accepted into the Choral Union, a two-hundred-voice all-college choir that performed three major oratorios every school year. Years later I told a friend, "Singing the Sanctus of Bach's *B-Minor Mass* with that outstanding chorus was almost as thrilling as a perfect orgasm." She didn't take me literally but caught my meaning.

In the spring of my sophomore year at Oberlin, I fell in love again. Tim Reed didn't mind my being slightly taller than he was. And, to me, his handsome face, dark curly hair and inquiring mind more than compensated for lack of height. To represent a pre-engagement commitment, he gave me a ring that had belonged to his grandmother—a pretty garnet mounted with two small diamonds. Because Tim lived near Detroit, we looked forward to seeing each other a few times over the summer before returning to Oberlin together the following fall.

Meanwhile, Suzie and I were encouraged by counselors to expand our horizons by rooming with different girls in the fall. Although we'd been happy living together for two years, we agreed to a change. Jeanne Aaronson, an oboe major in the Oberlin Conservatory of Music, was to be my junior year roommate. That summer after my sophomore year, however, my expectations for further college life and lasting love were shattered.

6

Relapse

THE WEATHER WAS HOT for June. What a blessing it was to be in Pentwater again. I planned to give myself a couple of weeks of swimming in Lake Michigan and lazing on the beach before looking for a summer job. My sophomore year at Oberlin College had been enriching, but demanding and tiring. I needed a break.

Little did I know what a long break I would have.

Before Doré and I were driven north by our friend David Hamberg, I had been through my usual lung checkup in Ann Arbor. The three of us were then joined in Pentwater by my current Oberlin boyfriend Tim Reed from Detroit and my college roommate Suzie with her fiancé Jim Burnett from Ohio. They all looked forward to celebrating Doré's birthday on June 20th.

That morning I was surprised by a long distance phone call.

"Judy, I'm so sorry to interrupt your vacation, but you need to come back to Ann Arbor as soon as you can," said

Dr. Marianna Smalley, our longtime family physician. "The specialists at the hospital want to take new X-rays," she explained. "They see a confusing shadow on your right lung, and they need to determine whether your lesion has re-activated."

After agreeing to return and hanging up the phone, I managed to process this shocking news before telling Doré what I'd learned.

"I sure hate to give you such a lousy birthday present," I sighed.

Our happily-anticipated restaurant celebration was rather subdued, but we weren't terribly worried. Surely new films would clear up any suspicions.

In the morning, I boarded the Greyhound bus for Ann Arbor, where I stayed with the family of Lilias Wagner. A friend since 7th grade, she was cheerfully supportive while we waited for the doctors to tell me there had been some mistake.

Two years earlier, when I entered Oberlin College, I had been protected by continuing pneumothorax treatments to keep my right lung collapsed and resting. Doctors at the University of Michigan Hospital had said that I could enjoy a normal campus life. "Normal," I assumed, meant a full social life in addition to meeting demanding academic requirements.

By summer, after my freshman year, those specialists decided that I had been recovered long enough that they could terminate the pneumos. Feeling liberated, I held my first paying job, behind the counter at the Pentwater Dairy Bar. Besides dishing up ice cream and serving sandwiches, I made new friends. I enjoyed days off at the beach, evening bonfires on the dunes and thrill rides at the annual Oceana County Fair—before returning to Oberlin in September.

Now, I suspected that the doctors' idea of "normal" meant a conscientiously cautious life for someone who'd had tuberculosis. Their advice may not have been carte blanche to burn the candle at both ends, as one commonly thinks of a typical student pace.

After reviewing a new set of X-rays, the doctors' faces were solemn. Instead of telling me they were mistaken about the shadow on my lung, they confessed that, in retrospect, the mistake had been discontinuing the protective pneumo treatments.

I braced myself.

The TB that had interrupted my life during high school had returned. So, instead of stretching out on a sunny beach, I was soon lying flat in bed again, on the 7th Floor of University of Michigan Hospital. I learned the hard way that this disease is never cured. It is only arrested.

This second confinement was even more distressing than my first go-'round, because I had a pretty good idea of how long I would be there. The prospect of giving up Oberlin, possibly never to return, was more than disappointing. It was devastating.

Although I could scarcely bear to imagine that, as before in my life, I accepted my fate and followed orders. I also insisted that my mother stay in Pentwater for the summer, as she had done when I had been hospitalized four years earlier. We both knew that there was nothing Doré could do for me by returning to the hot city. Wretched as she felt over what I faced, she agreed.

Rather than resume the pneumothorax treatments, the doctors decided to rest my lung another way.

"We are going to paralyze your diaphragm," said Dr. Jenkins. "We do that by pinching the phrenic nerve, which controls that movement."

"Where is *that*?" I blurted, astonished.

Responding gently, he explained, "There are two such nerves, one on each side at the base of the throat." Seeing that I understood, he continued, "We will make a small incision on the right side and simply crush the nerve. It should keep your diaphragm from moving, which will rest your lung and let the lesion heal."

When the anesthetic wore off, I was given pain-killing pills. The small wound only hurt for a week or so.

In most cases, I later learned, the phrenic nerve regenerated after a few months, so the surgery usually had to be repeated. No more than three operations were done, because the nerve might not revive. It was a short-term fix, but doctors believed it could help. I have a small scar as a reminder of my three procedures.

This time I was put in a two-bed room instead of a four-bed ward. My first roommate was Gudrun Knutson. In addition to her unusual name, her pale blonde hair revealed her Scandinavian heritage. Thin to the point of emaciation, "Goody" had been a student nurse when she came down with tuberculosis. Nurses were particularly susceptible to catching TB from patients they tended.

Believe it or not, "Goody" taught me to smoke.

From today's perspective, it is astonishing that medical science did not yet connect cigarettes with any sort of lung disease. Although I smoked off and on for years, often bumming from friends, I never lit up around my home or in an office, and didn't develop a serious habit. But my mother was a lifelong chain smoker. Imagine if she had contracted cancer in her remaining lung, after drastic surgeries collapsed the other one to treat her advanced TB.

Despite my determination to make the best of it, the relapse affected me even more dramatically than my first hospitalization. It became the most negative turning point of my life.

The impact began soon after I was forced to endure fulltime bed rest again, when my boyfriend wrote to ask me to mail back his grandmother's ring. Although Tim Reed lived in nearby Detroit, he never managed to visit me in the hospital, and his letters dwindled off. He didn't even come in person to request a return of the sweet garnet ring that had represented a pre-engagement commitment.

With stinging eyes, I read and re-read his letter.

"I'm not proud of myself," he wrote. "But I'm afraid of catching TB. If my education got interrupted, it might mean that I couldn't go to medical school."

I wondered if he really thought he would never come in contact with infectious diseases in medical school! I tried to understand his fears, but the shocking way he chose to break up with me almost broke my young heart. I tried to tell myself "good riddance," and keep a brave face forward, while silent tears soaked into my bed pillow.

Fortunately, several of my girlfriends visited often. Patsy Johnstone and Marilyn Dressel were faithful, sometimes bringing ice cream.

Another close friend, Lilias Wagner, managed to give me a real shampoo. A cooperative nurse wheeled a gurney beside my bed and helped me roll onto it, so that Lilias could push it across the hall to a large room that held several deep sinks. As I lay on my back, with my head stretched off one end of the gurney, she lathered and massaged my neglected scalp. Few sensations have equaled the pleasure that gave me. What a gift!

Years later, when my husband questioned my loyalty to a woman whose personality could be tiresome, I never failed to remind him of her kindness when I was hospitalized.

Another highlight was a late December visit from my Oberlin roommate Suzie and her bridegroom, Jim. They'd been married right after Christmas. She had expected me to be her maid of honor. Their decision to include Ann Arbor as a stop on their honeymoon is a heartwarming memory.

After Goody Knutson was released from the hospital, Stella Smith was the next patient to share my room. A plump brunette with a sweet round face, she, too, had to discontinue nurses training. Stella was already near the end of required bed rest by the time she was moved into my room, so she and I shared the wonder of doing more for ourselves.

After weeks of "dangling" and then "chair time" before walking, taking a tub bath instead of washing from a bedside basin, was a simple thrill. When we could walk in the hallway, we often used our "up time" marveling at the novelty of television, broadcast on a 7-inch screen in a neighboring ward.

After I went home, I frequently visited hospital patients who had become friends. Some of them were started on a new drug called Streptomycin. I had just missed that opportunity. Medical researchers had been trying to find a cure for TB for many years. Penicillin, the widely celebrated antibiotic, assailed a host of infections, but not tuberculosis. In 1943, Rutgers University scientist Selman Waksman discovered Streptomycin.

When compounded into a drug in 1944, it was hailed as a magic bullet, but it proved disappointing when the disease became resistant and tubercular patients regressed.

Finally, by the late 1940s, a combination of Streptomycin with other drugs worked well. I was happy for my friends, but I struggled against strong feelings of regret. My tuberculosis was never "active," i.e. contagious. Had the "drug cocktail" been made available to me at the time of my relapse, I could have stayed in college, with my activities restricted but not brought to a halt. I don't believe that dwelling on thoughts of "if only" is a healthy way to live, but sadness over that wasted period of my life arose now and then.

By the time I had lost another eleven months of my youth to TB, my sense of self-worth had completely eroded. At the age of 21, I felt like "damaged goods" with nothing to offer any boy. In 1950, the goal of almost any girl my age was to meet Prince Charming, get married and live happily ever after. This was the message we received from the national culture of the time. Most of us were the product—or the victims—of the post WWII years in America.

Women just a bit older had joined the WACS or the WAVES or had worked on factory assembly lines, making tanks and bombers. Personified as "Rosie the Riveter," their contributions to the war effort were lauded. But, when the soldiers and sailors came marching home, those women were told to give their jobs back to the men and find fulfillment in homemaking and motherhood. This post-war pressure was vigorously supported by commercial advertising, popular fiction and movies. By the time I was released from the hospital, I was an unwitting *slave* to that script.

Although my mother had traveled widely as a young woman, taught school after college and hadn't married until she was 27, Doré apparently accepted this new cultural norm. I knew that she and my grandparents expected me to finish my education somehow, but I don't remember her ever asking what I hoped to do after graduation other than marry.

I learned from letters, read years later, that she once told her sister Lurry there would be enough money in the trust fund created from my father's life insurance proceeds to cover my studies for an advanced degree. In 1950, she did not reveal that to me. I have sometimes wondered how I would have responded if she had. But I don't resent her decision. I believe that, at the time, she also assumed the relapse had narrowed my choices.

My physical activities were still sternly restricted that summer. Not only no swimming or square dancing, but doctors erroneously believed that the sun's rays would activate TB. I was not allowed to go to Pentwater beach, even for a cooling dip, until after 4:00 in the afternoon. Cradling my shattered self-image, I spent the greater part of each day reclining on the jazz couch—reading, writing letters, listening to music, sketching and longing for love.

I had no expectation of ever again living a normal life. Clearly, no prince would ever want such a handicapped wife. And no other future occurred to me.

馬

BOOK FOUR

THE FARMER TAKES A WIFE

"Peace.
It does not mean to be in a place
where there is no noise,
trouble or hard work.
It means to be
in the midst of those things
and still be calm
in your heart."

– Unknown

1

The Pentwater Yacht Club

"HI JUDY," said Joe Gamble, speaking through my front door screen. "My brother got tied up in a meeting after the dinner. He asked me to come give you a message."

I'd only met the two young men a few hours earlier at a spaghetti supper. Seeing my confusion, Joe hurried on, "Jim wondered if you'd go out with him Saturday night."

"Oh, I see," I said. "Uh… Yes. Tell him I'd like to." Trying to conceal how thrilled I was, I simply added, "Ask if he'll call me tomorrow night so I can explain my time concerns. OK?"

"Sure. Good. He'll do that," Joe said, as he backed away from my porch. "See you…"

"Thanks," I called after him. It was an unusual approach for a first date, but this was a Thursday, and Jim had to work Friday, so he risked it.

In August, 1950, Jim Gamble was living with his maternal grandmother, a prominent doyen of the resort village of Pentwater, Michigan, where my mother, Doré, and I spent our summers. The focus of seasonal social life was the Pentwater Yacht Club, which might sound upper crust, but few ritzy boats docked there. Most of the members just owned small sailboats—day sailers. Others, like Doré and friends, simply enjoyed the bar scene and dinners.

Thursday night spaghetti suppers drew casual crowds. When I'd been seated at a long table beside Jim and Joe Gamble, I'd learned that Jim was twenty-six, five years older than I was. He'd served in the Navy in the South Pacific during WWII and later took advantage of the G.I. Bill to earn a degree in horticulture from Michigan State University.

"This summer, I'm managing a fruit farm over in Hart, for an elderly widow, Mrs. Brooker," he told me. "It works out great for me to stay with my Grandma Diner. I can be some help to her in her old age, and it gives me a place to live 'til I can afford my own orchards." That was his goal.

I had no goals. I had been conditioned to please others. Even my academic achievements had been pursued in an effort to meet family expectations. By the time a relapse of TB forced me to leave Oberlin College and endure another year of hospitalization, I lacked any vision of a career or even any daydreams of the "happily ever after" future that most girls expected.

Moreover, my physical activities were still restricted that summer. Late afternoon swims were confined to brief dips in the water. Dancing, bowling or roller skating were forbidden, in order to keep my lung at rest. I had to spend long days alone on a built-in lounge Doré called "the jazz couch," as I'd done after my first hospitalization. I could read and sketch and listen to the radio, but I saw few people other than family friends. The Yacht Club supper was a treat.

My self-esteem still hadn't recovered, so Jim's attentions were flattering. He was a man—not a boy. An already receding hairline might have added to that impression. His friendly, open face was not fine-featured, but his warm, brown eyes were appealing. Standing about 5'11", he had a strong, lean physique that he maintained for the rest of his life.

What attracted me most to Jim that summer was that he was willing to simply hang out at home with me, listening to music and reading poetry aloud. His interest in my favorite pursuits was pleasantly surprising. He didn't seem to care that I couldn't go dancing or bowling or roller skating.

Reminiscing years later, Jim confessed. "I was tired after running around orchards all day. I had been driving a tractor, lugging ladders, supervising pickers and hauling cherries to the cannery. I had no time for swimming or lying around on a beach. And I was only too glad to meet a girl who didn't want me to take her dancing or bowling or roller skating."

When he finally told me that, we could laugh together at the irony of our separate expectations.

In September 1950, my mother and I returned to Ann Arbor, where she resumed her job at the University of Michigan, and I enrolled at U of M for my junior year of college. I could only take two courses at a time, and had to study at home in bed again, as I had in high school. So, I met few other students on campus and did not date.

Jim visited me as often as possible. In the fall he drove south overnight to bring truckloads of apples to sell at dawn in Detroit's Saturday morning Farmers' Market. Then he came over to Ann Arbor in the afternoon. I was sharing an apartment with Libby Myers, a graduate student employed as my mother's assistant in the U. of M. Art History Department. Her evening dates gave Jim and me time alone, and over the winter we convinced ourselves that we were in love. Inwardly, I knew that I was settling for less than head-over-heals romance, and Jim later told me that he had simply decided to love me because I was the kind of girl he wanted to marry. At least I felt loved, and that is what mattered to me then.

When I told my mother that we were thinking about a summer wedding, she asked, "Are you sure?"

"Of course, I'm sure," I declared. End of discussion.

If Doré had any reservations, she did not voice them to me. She knew I would manage to finish college. That was an imperative. All my family elders believed that whether or not a girl married, she should be able, in any future circumstance, to take care of herself.

In retrospect, it seems surprising that Doré didn't encourage me to postpone marriage, to pursue a career or to travel, as she had so loved doing in her youth. I learned long after her death that she was setting aside savings to allow me to go to graduate school.

She never revealed it, but apparently, she privately imagined that I would choose to enter some profession. Had she discussed it with me, it might have influenced my decisions. Yet in 1950, she probably shared my fear that I would never be fully healthy again. Jim told her that he was willing to do all the work around the house, if necessary, until I was fully recovered. In a letter to her sister, she expressed relief that a nice, steady, reliable man promised to take care of me.

"Jim is a kind, gentle guy, practical and capable, with his feet on the ground," my mother wrote. "And he has a complete understanding of Judy's physical limitations."

What she may not have understood was that, at twenty-one, I felt like an old maid. Girls in my generation were conditioned to think of marriage as a given. That winter, I had been a bridesmaid for two good friends. As astonishing as it seems to me today, I sensed life passing me by. Lacking an internal compass of my own, I followed Jim's.

Certainly, neither Doré nor I ever envisioned my marrying a farmer. But Jim was no country bumpkin. His maternal grandfather had been comptroller for the city of Detroit, and his grandmother was still a respected civic matron. While his father and uncle farmed, his paternal aunts and their husbands were teachers who played important roles in Jim's life after his mother's early death.

Family friend Walter Nelson, a Detroit attorney who introduced my parents to the summer resort of Pentwater back in 1931, described Jim as "the cream of Oceana County." At the time, it caused me to swell with pride. Years later it dawned on me that the boundaries of Oceana County did not exactly reach to far horizons, nor did it offer a world of choices. Still, that friend had also said, "You could go much further and find none finer than Jim Gamble."

It never occurred to me to look.

Our wedding date of August 18, 1951, was chosen for the brief break Jim would have "between peaches and apples." Of necessity, those two harvests dictated his schedule. A Unitarian minister friend of my father's conducted a brief afternoon ceremony in the Ann Arbor Congregational

Church, followed by a traditional cake-and-punch reception hosted by my step-grandmother at Skylodge, the Goss family mansion.

Jim's two brothers and a cousin were his groomsmen. My Oberlin roommate, Suzie, was my only attendant. A lace collar from the dress my mother wore in 1925 formed an inset in my simple handmade gown. Friends and family who traveled to share our big day included our four grandmothers, who had each played an important role in Jim's and my lives. Beloved aunts, uncles and cousins also came—along with dear friends.

After a driving trip in Ontario and two weeks at Aunt Ruth Gamble's cottage on the dunes north of Pentwater, I went back to Ann Arbor. Libby had arranged to move in with another friend in order to relinquish the apartment to the newlyweds. When Jim was able to join me there in November, he first worked installing television antennas before landing a job with the university's Psychology Department. While I carried five courses that winter, he helped to set up some significant scientific experiments. The light-tight rooms called "vision cubes" that he constructed were used to determine the best paint colors for school busses. We felt proud of his role in influencing government to switch from red-white-and-blue vehicles to the safer bright yellow.

On Christmas, he surprised me with a table-top crèche made from scrap plywood during his lunch hours. The paper maché figures he bought for the little stable reminded me of the miniature holy family, shepherds and wise men that I had played with as a child at my grandparents' home. It touched me that Jim remembered my description of that tradition. I was able to surprise him by learning to bake, and our party guests enjoyed my seasonal desserts and cookies.

In March, Jim moved back up north to start the spring farm work at the Booker place. The separation was hard on both of us. We hoped not to repeat that in the fall, so I sought and gained permission to complete my college degree requirements by correspondence. In June, I gave up the apartment and put our few furnishings in storage.

We spent the summer "camping out" in the old unfurnished house on the Brooker place. The widowed owner turned it over to us when she went to live with a daughter. Her late husband, Horace Brooker, had been a tightwad who installed electricity to the barn before the house and made do with whatever supplies he already owned before releasing a penny for anything more. The sink in the farmhouse kitchen was installed just two feet off the floor because that's as far as existing plumbing would reach. I sat on a milking stool to wash dishes.

Other than the low sink and a cooking range on another wall, a large wooden table in the center was the only object in the room. In the absence of any cabinets or counters, all the dishes, glassware, utensils, pots and pans, canned goods and packaged foods had to be kept on shelves in an adjoining pantry. An aged Kelvinator refrigerator stood in the back entryway. Roller skates might have helped. Had that occurred to me, my health was sufficiently improved by then to allow it.

We rolled a wringer washing machine into the kitchen, where one hose was hooked up to fill it and another positioned to drain the water into the sink after the washing cycle. Then it could be refilled to rinse the load. At least it was electric. Clothes had to be hand-fed into the wringers, but I was grateful that I didn't have to use a washboard in a tub or take garments down to a stream to pound them on rocks.

Needless to say, I did not expect to start married life in such circumstances. But I began my on-the-job training cheerfully, not only creating enticing meals but learning to can vegetables and fruits, jellies and jams. My chili sauce won a blue ribbon at the Oceana County Fair.

A July highlight was the annual Pirate's Ball. As Doré described the evening in a letter to her sister, "Judy wore an off-the-shoulder white cotton blouse with an old blue chambray skirt that she'd cut and ripped to look ragged along the hem and high on one thigh. Lots of jangly jewelry completed the costume. She sewed a black eye patch for Jim and made him up to look properly menacing under a red bandana, with a fake dagger tucked into his belt… And they were voted Pirate King and Queen!"

For many years to come, my mother "sat" our babies while we danced the Pentwater Yacht Club.

2

Juniper Orchards

"WELL, the *location* is just beautiful," said my mother, gazing off beyond orchards and across verdant fields toward dense woods. She had come from Ann Arbor to spend her spring vacation with us and have her first look at our new home. Jim and I were excited to have a place of our own.

After our newlywed summer and fall of 1951 at Mrs. Brooker's, Jim and his brother Joe formed a partnership to buy a large fruit farm near the village of Mears, six miles west of Hart. Joe had followed Jim in earning a college degree in horticulture at Michigan State University, and the brothers looked forward to working together.

The 420 total acres included 230 acres in orchards— apples, cherries, peaches, pears and plums. Because the setting was less than a mile from Juniper Beach on Lake Michigan, we called our farm "Juniper Orchards." At the time it didn't occur to us that some folks would think we produced evergreens rather than fruit.

The property also included nearly a hundred acres of woods, with horse trails we leased to a neighboring riding stable. The arrangement also allowed us to ride without charge when demand was low. During the years ahead, I never tired of the view from the kitchen window, across meadows where horses grazed, to those inviting woods.

That first spring, as my mother and I stood in the front yard with our backs to the farmhouse, she stalled for time by shaking a cigarette from her red leather case. I'd tooled it for her during the second winter I spent recovering from TB. Doré rarely said anything that I might take as criticism, but I could almost always read her. So I was aware that she was keeping her opinions of our new home to herself.

The house was old and tired. Rooms were small and dark. As soon as we moved in, Jim and I began stripping wallpaper, painting walls and woodwork and planning some structural changes. Although she may have sighed inwardly over all the work ahead, Doré soon assured me that she could see the possibilities.

"I'm hoping we can remove the wall between the little downstairs bedroom and the so-called parlor to create one large living room," I told her.

"Oh, that would be wonderful—so much more spacious and lighter." She was clearly relieved to look beyond its present state.

I knew she could envision the plan. Twenty years earlier, she had remodeled her summer home in nearby Pentwater, ripping off the decaying front porch, adding a large white brick fireplace and built-in bunks and closets. Finished with rosy pink woodwork and deep blue floors, that house testified to her creative imagination and eye for potential changes. I took the decor for granted, growing up, but now I had reason to remember that she was the one who planned and supervised that transformation.

Our kitchen wasn't as bad as the one on the Brooker farm, but still pretty dismal. The sink was a normal height, but solitary. To compensate for the lack of surrounding counter tops, I used a straight-backed wooden chair to hold an upended apple crate topped with a Rubbermaid dish rack and draining tray that directed rinse water into the sink. At least, on an opposite wall, a floor-to-ceiling built-in cabinet held dishes and canned goods. No more trips to an adjoining pantry.

While my days were primarily focused on housework, I felt pleased to be entrusted with the role of "pay mistress" in the orchards during harvest. For each lug of cherries brought to me, I gave the picker two quarters.

Every summer, migrant workers returned to Michigan from their Texas homes to pick green beans in southern counties and fruit up north. In retrospect, fifty cents a lug doesn't sound like much, but entire families worked, and over a day and a week, their cash amounted to—enough.

Their livelihood depended on ours, so our relationship was friendly. The concrete block quarters we provided were sparsely furnished but easy to keep clean. The crew boss was an alcoholic, and a few women were clearly victims of domestic violence, but they didn't speak of it. Nor did I.

Only two incidents mar my memories of those families. Once, when we were not at home, the crew boss needed to use our telephone. Drunk as usual, he climbed in through the low window at the end of the kitchen, putting all his considerable weight on the end of our dinette table. We were never able to repair the broken support for the leaf.

The other occurrence hurt my heart. My childhood doll house, made by my late father, was stored in the big barn for future use by the daughter I hoped to have. In each room, a small cardboard carton held the furniture for that space. After the pickers had moved on at the end of one fruit season, I discovered that all the little boxes had been stolen. I am the only one who remembers the tiny standing radio, grand piano, refrigerator with coils on the top and other miniatures of the 1930's. At least we still had the house. My two daughters and four granddaughters have enjoyed several incarnations of furnishings and color schemes.

Despite those two incidents on the farm, my acquaintance with workers of Mexican descent gave me an appreciation for their rich cultural heritage and the demands of their way of life. Remembering that today, I realize that knowing those workers gave me a valuable background for understanding the current controversies over Latino immigration.

As the mistress of Juniper Orchards, I threw myself into rural domesticity. Jim joined the Pomesters, a fruit growers' association, and we both became members of the local Farm Bureau chapter. From a neighbor, I learned what was expected when we took our turn hosting a monthly meeting. "You'll need to serve a lunch," Mrs. Flood said.

"At the end of the evening?" I asked incredulously.

"Oh yes. People will expect it."

"You mean just a dessert?" I said with hope.

"Oh, no. They'll want sandwiches and Jello salads plus cake and pie."

It amazed me that the men and their wives could consume all that at 10 p.m. Maybe they'd skipped supper.

In the 1950s, the competition to surpass other hostesses in the quality of luscious desserts was a given. Some of my most popular offerings were a pumpkin cake with fluffy caramel frosting and chocolate "ice box cake," a recipe I'd begged from my step-grandmother "Mom Goss." A Gamble family favorite was sour cream pie, full of an egg custard with plumped raisins and flavored with powdered cloves. Jim once told me that his grandmother had judged me worthy of joining the family when I baked that correctly. Excellent fruit pies were required.

I also prepared food for Couples Club of the Congregational Church, a women's Child Study Club and the Hart Hospital Auxiliary. When I was elected president of the auxiliary, I spent hours fund raising, presiding over meetings and attending health care conferences. Then Doré's sighs became audible. She simply couldn't understand what made me tick! She had always derided people she called "Causey Women." Never in her life did she join any organization, and she despaired of knowing why I wanted to spend so much time on what she considered pointless pursuits.

Her disdain hurt, but, at that time, neither of us accounted for my low self-esteem and strong need for others' approval. It fed my ego to be entrusted with such responsibilities.

Although my mother rejected organized religion, she did like hearing me sing solos with the church choir. We had joined the Hart church for the music as well as friendships. And Doré was proud when I learned to use a sewing machine and saved money by making garments for myself and our daughter Jennifer, born in June 1954. I even replaced zippers—

notably in a red wool hunting jacket!

Meanwhile, Jim agreed to work on our house's possibilities. He knew that I had envisioned creating a large living room by combining the parlor and the equally dark small bedroom.

"Can we take out the wall between those rooms" I asked, untying my apron.

"I think so, as long as it's not load-bearing," Jim answered. "Where would the desk go?" He had been using the bedroom as an office.

"How about putting it at the east end of the new room?" I wondered.

"Sure. Your dad's Chinese desk is so good looking, it would be nice to have it out in the main room where other people can see it." Jim was grateful to Doré for letting him have that handsome heirloom. It was rarely used in the Pentwater study, and it pleased her to see it at our farm.

Apparently realizing what the proposed change would require of him, he said, grinning, "I'll do my best to keep it neat."

"Oh good," I rushed on, sensing his cooperative mood. "Now, what would you think of installing a big picture window in the west wall? It would bring in lots more light and frame our wonderful view of the meadow and woods."

"Sure! That sounds doable, and I agree it would look great."

"And, while you're at it, how about walling over the old front door?"

Chuckling, Jim said, "Good idea! No one ever comes in that way—unless it's some guy selling encyclopedias."

The resulting room, created by Jim and his brothers, made an amazing difference in the whole feel of the house.

Inviting and comfortable, it easily accommodated after-dinner guests and the groups we entertained. Furnished with a few other Chinese antiques, a scroll painting, Japanese prints and some colorful reproductions, our living room drew many compliments.

Upstairs, Jim built a closet in our bedroom, and the second front room eventually became a nursery. Later, in a slant-ceilinged attic space over the back of the house, he created a playroom for our children.

...

The whole family was proud when the Chamber of Commerce named Jim the "Outstanding Young Farmer" of 1957 in Oceana County and a state finalist. But a few years of killing frosts and low fruit prices compelled Jim to add to our farm income. For a year he taught 4th, 5th and 6th graders in a local two-room schoolhouse. Farm record- keeping and school lesson planning competed for his evenings, and he was required to take courses to earn his teacher's certificate. I was pleased to be supportive by helping with his college art projects and by directing the school children's Christmas program.

It was fun guiding the kids through making props and learning lyrics to present "The Twelve days of Christmas" for their parents and grandparents.

It was a low blow to discover that to earn a teaching certificate, Jim was expected to go back on campus for one semester. "That means a term without any income at all," Jim said. "I'd have to rent a room in Lansing. And I don't know how we can cover that and whatever you'll need here."

"It will also mean my managing alone with two little kids," I pointed out.

"Yeah," he sighed. "That could be risky for you, 'specially without a car. I'd like to be able to drive home weekends, but that would cost money, too...."

As I thought about all this, Jim went on to explain, "I've also been wondering whether trying to combine farming and teaching is really going to work out."

It took a while to talk it out, but we had to face it. With the apple harvest continuing into November and orchard spraying beginning again in March, the conflicting schedules made the combination much more demanding than simply adding a "winter job." Reluctantly, we agreed to take our chances on the fruit crops and "tighten our belts," as Jim said, until our orchards could fully support us without his teaching.

I learned so much as a farmer's wife that I would have never known otherwise. Not only can I describe the popular varieties of cherries, apples and peaches, I know where they grow best. I learned what it is like to live at the mercy of the weather. If an early spring that brings premature blossoms is followed by a late frost, the whole crop can literally be nipped in the bud. Heavy rainfall while ripe fruit is hanging on the trees causes sweet cherries to swell and split. That means accepting a lower price at the cannery rather than selling little baskets to tourists.

Birds are as hazardous to fruit farmers as weevils to corn growers. Extended droughts cannot always be counteracted by irrigation. Even bountiful harvests are problematic. Too many truckloads of fruit pulling through the gates of the canneries mean lower prices.

A poignant illustration of our precarious financial position was a note I wrote to Doré in a Mother's Day card. I told her we couldn't buy the copper-clad sauce pan she wanted, because Taylor Hardware in Hart was sold out of them and it was the only store where we could charge the purchase. "We have *no* cash right now." I said. "But as soon as some people pay up what they owe us we will get it and have it waiting for you in Pentwater in June. I know you understand, but I hate having to *ask* you to."

In 1960, Jim's statewide prominence as an outstanding young farmer led to a job as a sales representative for a firm that manufactured agricultural chemicals. We were relieved and concerned. It would mean regular paychecks, but it would require a move north. How could he still operate our farm?

Although Jim's brother Joe was still a co-owner, he had already left the farm to earn a doctorate at Purdue and take a research job at Michigan State in East Lansing. The brothers decided to hire a manager for Juniper Orchards, and Jim and I moved our family to Traverse City.

Although I missed natural setting of our farm, I relished the cultural advantages and better schools our family would enjoy. A popular tourist destination, the city is also the year-round home to well-educated professional people who brought the arts to the north woods. While pointing with pride to the National Music Camp and the subsequent Interlochen Arts Academy, only twenty miles away, they went on to establish a community college and symphony orchestra.

Jim was fully qualified for his new job as a territory manager for Niagara Chemical Company, a division of FMC

Corporation. Our first year in Traverse City, Jim drove two hours each way to spend weekends working the farm. But his boss objected to his divided attention. Eventually, the brothers made the difficult decision to sell Juniper Orchards. It was painful for Jim to give up his lifetime dream of owning his own farm, but he didn't talk about it—not until many years later.

During his years of selling pesticides and fungicides in Michigan's northern Lower Peninsula, I learned to expect early morning phone calls.

"It rained last night," a fruit grower would say. "Am I right to worry about apple scab? What should I spray on my orchards?" And then, "How soon can you deliver it?"

I was amused to note that Jim was as important to his customers as a country doctor to expectant mothers.

...

We never read poetry aloud again. Yet I hold no regrets about the choices of my youth.

Jim and I divorced, but our incompatibility had nothing to do with his being a farmer. I always admired his strong work ethic and how hard he strived to succeed in his chosen field and support his family.

After I was self-supporting and our children were grown, Jim and I each happily remarried. We not only wished each other well, we acknowledged that our early lives had been enriched by the years that followed the day the farmer took a wife.

3

Claim to Fame

THE PHONE CALL CAME right at dinner time.

We almost didn't answer it, because we had just served our houseguests, two couples from Ann Arbor vacationing in western Michigan that 1953 Labor Day weekend.

But it might be important. So I picked up the phone.

"Good evening," purred the disembodied male voice. "I represent the Pinkerton Detective Agency. Did you submit an entry in the Crosley Appliance Company's 'Plan Your Dream Kitchen' contest?"

"Ye—sss. Why?" I stammered, questioning my ears.

"You have been selected as one of the first prize winners," said the detective, matter-of-factly. "Our agency has been asked to visit your home to verify your entry......"

Excitement and panic chased each other around in my mind as he continued to explain. I finally tuned in again in time to hear him ask, "Would tomorrow morning be convenient for you?"

"Of course….." I managed to say, and in shock, I gave him driving directions to our fruit farm—six miles from the town of Hart and less than a mile from the shores of Lake Michigan.

I hadn't forgotten the contest. Not after all the hours of dreaming and designing to present my vision of an ideal kitchen in our forty-year-old white frame farmhouse. But, of course, I had squelched any hope of actually winning a nationwide competition.

Now, when it sounded as if the dream might be coming true, I faced an immediate obstacle. The space I had drawn on my contest form was actually a combination of two areas—the old kitchen and a back shed! An outside wall separated the two. The detective's words were sinking in. He was coming to determine if I was, indeed, the person who submitted the plan, AND he was coming to see the house! He had to verify whether the space I described truly existed—and as of that moment, it did not.

Dinner was accompanied by endless questions and excited chatter as everyone let the news sink in. I answered the others' questions about how I had heard about the contest—in a magazine—and what the contest required—meticulous measuring, drawing old and new floor plans, hand painting, and then pasting cutouts of Crosley equipment on the fold-out wall elevations. But, as I accepted their congratulations, utter turmoil raged inside. How in the world would I be able to persuade the detective to imagine one large sunny room where he saw only two small unrelated areas?

When I finally admitted what was on my mind, one of our guests, Jay, an engineer, dismissed my concerns with a wave. "Oh, that's simple," he declared. "We'll just tear the wall down!"

"Of course!" answered his friend, Randy, as Jim gratefully accepted their help.

The six of us worked through the night. The men tore off exterior siding and interior plaster and lath; chain sawed through thick studs and moved them over to create a new wall dividing the old shed. Half of the shed would become part of the kitchen; the other half eventually became a rear entry and utility room.

As the men tossed down boards and hunks of old plaster wall, Jeanne, Sally and I hauled the debris away to a pile behind the nearby garage/machine shop. The men hammered a new partition into place while we women swept up the dust and rolled a hunk of old patterned linoleum rug over the marks on the floor that would otherwise reveal the location of the former kitchen wall. Once we had moved a table and chairs into the newly created "breakfast area," the space began to look as I had imagined it.

The shed end of the room was rustic, but not totally out of character with the kitchen itself. The "before" pictures taken by a photographer who came with the Pinkerton detective, showed the old floor-to-ceiling cupboards, the 1915 white and black electric stove with its skinny curving legs and high oven on one side, and the narrow wall-hung porcelain sink. Beside the sink stood a rickety wooden chair on which an upended apple crate, topped by a rubber dish rack and tray, served as a drainboard. A small, enamel-topped table offered the only work surface.

Cinderella was about to go to the ball.

The 100 second prize winners in the Crosley "Plan Your Dream Kitchen" contest received their choice of one kitchen appliance. As a first prize winner, I was to receive an entire kitchen, exactly as I had designed it, using Crosley equipment—including the deep freezer I longed for, the latest style in heavy white metal cabinets with molded red vinyl countertops, display shelves, a tuck-away rolling cart, and such modern innovations as an electric dishwasher. The detective notarized my signature on a document promising to install everything. Apparently winners of previous contests sold their new possessions.

A $500 cash allowance covered the installation. Because Jim and his brothers Joe and Jack were able to do most of that work, the money helped to pay for a new picture window in the breakfast area, relocating a door from the dining room, and creating wooden soffit cabinets above the white metal ones.

The newspaper photograph of me accepting the check from the local Crosley appliance dealer shows a beaming, misty-eyed young housewife who hardly knew what hit her! And there were more surprises to come.

Just as the basic remodeling was completed and we were about to paint the walls before cabinets and appliances were installed, I received another astonishing phone call. *Redbook* magazine had decided to do a photo feature on one of the 100 first prize winners in the Crosley contest—and they had picked ME!! What, I wondered, had determined their choice?

Unlike the original contest judges, who had been impressed by accuracy in measurement, precision in the use of cutouts representing the Crosley equipment, and clever use of space, the magazine editors were looking for a human-interest angle.

They were smitten by the detective's "before" pictures!

Their concept was to dramatize the transformation in the life of a farm wife who had no kitchen counters and managed to drain dishes from a fruit crate. Because they romanticized the whole idea of coming out from Manhattan to Michigan to do the photo shoot, they took over the decorating—completely.

When Jack McCurdy, Redbook's features editor, called to ask if there was an airport in Mears, I had to inform him that the nearest runway was in Muskegon, 45 miles away. "What do I do then?" he yelled.

Amused, I answered, "Well, I guess you just take a bus to Hart, call me from there and we will pick you up." He gulped as I wondered if he had ever been farther west than Twelfth Avenue.

As we waited for his call on the appointed day, Mr. McCurdy rode up to our rural mailbox in a yellow cab, which he had taken for 85 miles from Grand Rapids, and kept waiting for two hours while he looked over our home and explained that a decorator would be suggesting the color scheme that the magazine would dictate for my kitchen.

Not knowing an apple tree from a cherry tree when he arrived, the sophisticated New Yorker clearly expected to be bored silly on a fruit farm in the wilds of Western Michigan. So it was a pleasant surprise to discover that instead of country bumpkins, Jim and I were articulate college graduates. And instead of butter churns and spinning wheels, our home was furnished with Asian antiques. After admiring our carved camphor wood chest and hanging scrolls, he took his cab back to Grand Rapids.

In the weeks that followed, every mail delivery seemed to bring more paint chips and fabric swatches. The dark red countertops were to be complemented by coral pink walls! PINK! In a kitchen? In 1953?! I could just imagine the reaction to that in our rural community! Furthermore, the chair seats were to be upholstered in chartreuse, and the end wall near the dining room was to be paneled in "pecky" cypress!

"Who on earth would want that worm-eaten wood indoors?" exclaimed the local carpenter who helped Jim install it.

It wasn't difficult to relinquish control of the color scheme, because the magazine arranged with famous manufacturers who *donated* all the products and furnishings in return for acknowledgment in the article. Armstrong provided the spatter-pattern linoleum. Daystrom gave us the modern black Formica table with tubular metal chairs and matching bar stools. Lightolier lighting company donated an elegant pull-down fixture with slatted wood shade to hang over the table, and Martin-Senour Company contributed the paint. The window curtains, made to order by Jofa, featured a large fruit print design in subtle earth colors with pink, at the then unimaginable cost of $7.50 a yard!! A beautiful modern wall clock came from the Howard Miller Company, and Corning Ware baking dishes completed the scene.

After Jim and his brothers completed the remodeling, we gave the walls two coats of the prescribed pink paint and installed the appliances and cabinets—finishing just in time for the magazine interview and photo shoot. An April date was set during one of my frequent phone conversations with Jack McCurdy and with Ruth Fairchild Pomeroy, the homemaking editor. I reserved motel rooms for them and for the photographer and a home economist from Dow Corning who came along to create a picture-perfect meal that would show off her company's casserole dishes.

Shortly after their arrival, the ample features editor, who already affected a rumpled journalist style, loosened his tie, folded his corduroy clad arms across his broad chest and gazed contentedly beyond a meadow and stream to distant woods. "I could get used to this," he sighed.

Before long, the slim, smoothly-coifed homemaking editor slipped out of her high-heeled pumps and left her condescending demeanor on a hanger with her peach silk suit jacket. The Chinese photographer enjoyed hearing that my parents had lived in his homeland. We all hit it off amazingly well—until the Dow-Corning home economist messed up—literally.

The magazine editors had conceived a typical farm supper, featuring a tasteless "Country Meat Loaf" that called for a package of frozen mixed vegetables and tomato soup added to unseasoned ground beef. The dessert was "Milk and Honey Apple Tart," equally bland but edible. The recipes for these two dishes were published in the magazine article as two of my favorites. If they had *asked me* I probably would have given them beef stroganoff or lamb curry, neither of which would have fit their profile of a farmer's wife!!

Rounding out the menu was a casserole of scalloped potatoes, to be baked, of course, as were the meat loaf and apple tart, in the smart contemporary Corning Ware. Little did we know what a disaster lay ahead.

While the photographer talked with me about photo angles in the spotless new kitchen, the home economist and the Redbook homemaking editor prepared the food in the utility room, on top of my brand new Sears electric washer. Neither of those career women thought to ask me

147

for a cutting board, so for the next 20 years, scars on my washing machine were a constant reminder of where they sliced the onions and potatoes!

Worse yet, when the editor was called away into the kitchen, to consult on the photo shoot, the home economist decided that one dish of scalloped potatoes was enough, and that the other one would just be for show. So she crumpled aluminum foil in the bottom of the casserole, sliced a few potatoes on top for effect, and left the utility room. When the editor returned, she helpfully finished the food preparation by adding milk to both casserole dishes. If she wondered why it took so much liquid to fill the second one, I never heard. But, later, when the whole meal was baked in my pristine Crosley oven, the milk boiled over into a blackened crust on the unprotected new bottom surface. The photographer was glad that the smoke clouded the room *after* his work was done. The predictable mess was left for me to clean up when the whole crew had departed.

The photographer was a pro. In addition to shots of the decor and equipment, he was asked to take pictures of me which didn't reveal that I was seven months pregnant! The magazine provided a blouse, apparently on the assumption that I would own nothing suitable, and, to cover my skirt, they gave me a gathered apron made of fabric that matched the curtains. Thus attired, I was posed seated at the new table or standing with my arm draped artfully across my body as if pointing out the features of the home freezer. No one would guess that my first-born child was on her way.

The subterfuge was not limited to concealing the pregnancy and inventing homey recipes. Objective Truth, I soon learned, does not matter to big name magazines.

When editors make up their minds about what constitutes a good story, don't confuse them with the facts. Ours was a fruit farm. We didn't raise herds of cattle or vast acres of hay. But the article published the following September described my life as if I fed twenty-five neighboring threshers every noon.

It was embarrassing. But our real neighbors understood. And when they flocked to the open house we hosted after the New Yorkers flew home, most folks even grudgingly acknowledged that the pink walls didn't look all that bad. When one woman sighed with envy, her husband grumbled, "Remember, Betty, Jim didn't *buy* all this stuff for Judy. You go win a contest and you can have it too."

The unique décor of my prize kitchen turned out to be a delight to live and work in. Many a Mason jar of homegrown peaches and tomatoes cooled on the long red Crosley countertops. Two babies learned to crawl on that easy-to-clean Armstrong linoleum floor. And the Daystrom dinette set was used for school homework, letter-writing and farm record-keeping, as well as family meals for years to come.

4

Great Expectations

THE PAGES OF MY DAYS would hardly be complete without some reflections on having children.

The topic of Motherhood (capital M) has evoked volumes of sappy sentiment or vitriolic vengeance. Has any researcher counted the number of pages (or recent blogs) devoted to women's tear-streaked reminiscences or regrets? Most feature dramatic descriptions of raising children into adulthood. This chapter won't. Just the beginnings.

My feelings about having children arose in reaction to my mother's attitudes. She bore me only because my father wanted an heir. Had their firstborn child lived more than a few hours, I wouldn't have been conceived. She never let me forget that.

And, because of my father's fragile health, their choice to stop at one healthy child also shaped my life. As an only offspring, I was often among grown-ups and treated as a miniature adult. As I grew, I concluded that an ideal family would consist of two boys and two girls. As it happened, that turned out to be my reality.

...

My first pregnancy was precisely timed. Jim and I wanted to wait to welcome a baby until after I finally earned my college degree and we were happily settled in our farmhouse. By the time our daughter arrived on June 10, 1954, the house also included a sparkling new prize-winning kitchen.

While we were expecting, everyone in Jim's family hoped for a girl. Jim was the oldest of six sons, so it seemed natural that his dad and aunts and uncles, who mattered greatly in his life, wanted us to play another suit.

We called her Jennifer because I loved the name. Most family members and friends assumed that we picked it to continue the tradition of the first initial. Jim's brothers were named Joe, Jack, John, Jeff and Jerre. And then Jim married Judy. But, quite truthfully, it had not occurred to us that our child's name *should* start with J. Few believed us.

Jenni was a beautiful baby, with a head of strawberry blonde fuzz. My friend Libby Myers called her "your little pink-haired girl," a nickname that my daughter and I still chuckle over now and then.

As an avid advocate for natural childbirth and breastfeeding, I drew deep pleasure from nursing our daughter. Besides cuddling the soft warmth of her body, I loved the quiet interludes spent inhaling the scent of her little head and listening to her eager sucking. She thrived without ever having a bottle. She willingly drank orange juice from a small cup early on, so when she was nine months old, it was easy to wean her directly to milk in the cup.

Jim agreed that he did not want Jenni to be an only child, so we didn't wait long to get pregnant again. We hoped for a boy and lucked out.

But our son's timing was less than convenient. Jim's brother Jack and his wife Nancy were living in a smaller house on our farm. When we phoned them about 2 a.m. to say that my labor had started, they had just gone to bed after a Saturday night party. Groggily, they stumbled across the road to stay with Jenni while Jim drove me the six miles to Oceana County Hospital in Hart. I think the three of them got some sleep before dawn.

Meanwhile, our baby made a dramatic appearance— backwards. His little bottom was trying to emerge where his head should have been.

"Don't push," yelled Dr. John Vrbanac.

Startled by this loud command from a normally mild-mannered physician, I held my breath and obeyed. He reached his gloved hand up inside me and turned the slippery infant around.

"Okay. Now push," he quietly instructed me.

After a successful conclusion, John pulled down his surgical mask and explained. "The first baby I ever delivered, as an intern, was a breach birth. I broke its arm. That's made me a little nervous at such times ever since." Shoving back his cotton cap and wiping his forehead, he added, "I'm sorry I yelled at you."

"It's okay," I murmured. Exhausted as I was, I wanted

him to know that I understood the risks he faced. "You knew exactly what to do," I told him. "Thank you."

I'll never forget the profound happiness I felt a little later that Sunday morning—February 26, 1956—as I finally reclined against soft white bed pillows, watched whopping snowflakes fall silently outside the window, and held our wee son—Christopher James Gamble.

Once more, our baby's name drew strange comments. We thought the obvious move away from the initial letter J would satisfy folks.

But one friend said, "Oh isn't that cute!"

Isn't <u>what</u> cute?" I asked.

"Well—JenniFER and ChristoPHER. They sort of rhyme or whatever."

Give us a break, I thought.

...

Again, I enjoyed nursing the baby but was no longer a purist about it. If Jim and I left him with my mother for an evening, I didn't rush back in the middle of a Yacht Club dance to feed him. Instead, Doré gave him a bottle of breast milk that I had pumped out in advance.

Jenni was a devoted big sister, devising endless ways to amuse the baby—who grew into a mellow little boy. She began kindergarten in the rural West Golden Township two-room school where Jim had been teaching grades 4, 5 and 6. Smart and friendly, she excelled. And when we moved to Traverse City in December 1959, she merged right in with her class in the neighborhood elementary school just a block from our small rented house. Both children seemed to accept and adjust to the new home and community.

At ease in new surroundings, Chris once wandered away from me in a department store. After long guilty minutes of searching, I finally spotted him sitting cross-legged on the floor between rows of towering book shelves. Looking up calmly, surprised by my anxiety, he told me, "You should have 'membered I'm a book looker."

I was glad about the move to a widely-respected city where our family would have more cultural and educational advantages. I gradually became active in the arts community.

But that first year, Jim was busy establishing a customer base for the agricultural chemicals he sold, and he was spending every weekend back on the farm, overseeing the hired man. So the kids and I were isolated and adrift. Jenni and Chris began to drive me crazy with their jealous squabbling. Yelling or shrieking, they produced unceasing din.

I decided that what we all needed was a *new baby*.

What was I *thinking*?

Still stuck in a 1950s mentality, thinking had little to do with it. In those rigid days, unhappy women had few ways to lift their spirits. Unless they ran away from home, they usually chose between bleaching their hair and having another baby. Although both my children would soon be in school, it absolutely never entered my mind that I might look for a job. And I honestly thought that the kids would delight in a sweet infant and quit fighting with each other.

My mother so disapproved of my choice that she was cold and disengaged throughout my pregnancy. Fortunately,

I was kept busy planning and carrying out another move. After a year of renting, Jim and I decided to buy an old white frame house on the more established west side of town.

Our second daughter, Cynthia, was born on February 13, 1961, in the large regional hospital a few blocks away. Breastfeeding again went well, until her teeth came in before she was four months old. When she began biting, I abandoned my principles, switched to formula and fed her from bottles—with no adverse effect on her health. With curly auburn hair and grey-green eyes, Cyndi was an adorable child, who charmed all within her sphere—including her grandmother.

Tent camping was a special treat. Not only did it permit inexpensive vacations, it gave Jim permission to play. If he was teaching outdoor skills or fishing, he could relax and stop worrying about chores. The girls and I created a camp kitchen with custom fitted fruit crates. We all relished simple suppers cooked on the Coleman stove, particularly when dessert was s'mores melted over campfires.

Singing in the car relieved the drive home. A favorite was "I see the moon and the moon sees me…"

Summers also included many happy days in Pentwater at Grammy Doré's house and Aunt Ruth Gamble's and Uncle Kenney's cottages on the dunes north of the village. We all loved the Lake Michigan beach as much as I had as a child.

Jim and I felt that our family was complete. With full hands, we shelved old visions of having "a bunch of kids," and life was good.

But, three years later, a failure of contraception found us pregnant again. *Devastated* is not too strong a word to describe my emotions when Dr. Fishbeck confirmed my suspicion.

"Relax," he said. "This is the child who will grow up to be President of the United States."

Easy for you to say, I thought. The prospect of having another baby left me shaking with dread. While mothering three beautiful children held deep satisfaction for me, I felt stretched. We couldn't afford household help, much less a nanny. How would I manage with four?

Leaving the doctor's office with a supply of pre-natal vitamins, I considered my alternatives. In those days before Roe v. Wade, Dr. Fishbeck could not legally perform an abortion, even if willing. I had three other choices. One would be to find some sleazy, back alley doctor operating illegally in Detroit. The second would be to drive from Michigan to Mexico for an equally unsanitary operation. The third choice was a last resort left to women who could not even afford the first two: a wire coat hanger. Each choice often ended a woman's life as well as her baby's. I chose inertia.

A strange premonition also contributed to my lack of action. Not one to harbor superstitions, I began to have freaky fears. It was irrational, but I believed that if I terminated the new life budding within me, harm would come to one of our other children. Maybe even death.

I couldn't do it.

To my relief, my mother understood my distress. She was supportive this time, as I suffered in elastic stockings during one of Michigan's hottest summers. My Aunt Lurry spent her Pentwater vacation helping Doré to cope with the daily needs of Jenni, Chris and Cyndi while we all waited for a baby who was two weeks late. By his arrival on a sweltering August 14, 1964, he'd put on extra weight. At 8 lbs. 14 ounces, he was the largest of our infants, and the first to have his father's dark brown eyes. We named him Scott Benjamin Gamble. The arrival of a second son balanced our family to the two boys and two girls that I had dreamed of in my youth. I would manage.

When we brought Scotty home, I placed him in one of the most gorgeous bassinettes any baby ever had. A friend, Diane Deknatel Davis and her husband Roger had lived in the Philippines when their son Paul was born. That boy began life in the large white wicker basket, on wheeled legs, covered by a floor-length lace-trimmed fine cotton skirt and matching high hood. Later, their daughter Roxanne slept in this magnificent little bed, before her parents lent it to us.

Although Scott Ben's birth resulted from an "unwanted pregnancy," it gave us all a precious infant and toddler who became a handsome, talented, deeply beloved little boy.

5

Of Ironing Boards and Ovens

STEPHANIE, my eldest adult granddaughter, not only raised her voice in astonishment, she then sat with her mouth open.

"You mean that ironing boards were all the same height when you were young? I can't imagine having to bend way over! Or what if you were really short? Would you have to stand on a stool to iron?

"Yep."

Acknowledging, in the spring of 2014, that neither of us ironed clothes very often, we shared our appreciation for contemporary fabrics. But Stephanie was still genuinely interested in learning when manufacturers conceived of adjustable ironing boards. Because of a major event in my own life, I knew exactly.

Back in the 1950's, when I lived on a fruit farm, my fame as "the Mrs. Gamble who won a national kitchen planning contest" led to some local acclaim. I did wonder, when asked to judge cherry pies at the county fair, what designing had to do with baking. But apparently most folks felt that certain aspects of homemaking were connected. Good at one, good at all.

For bathroom design, in a McCall's Magazine contest, my honorable mention award was a set of luxurious towels. I could never have conceived of what would follow.

In August, 1957, I received a letter from the magazine, inviting me to be a delegate to its first Women's Congress on Better Living. As one of 100 women from all over the United States, I was being asked to attend a three-day conference October 9-11 in Washington, D.C.

Wow! Why me? I thought.

In the letter, Mary Davis Gillies, the "Houses and Home Fashions" editor, wrote, "Over the years that we have been conducting room decorating contests, I feel that I have come to know you through your entries. Now, because of your talent for home planning and design, we would like to have your help.

"The purpose of this congress," she went on to say, "is to help us determine what women most want in their homes of today and tomorrow as a result of new living patterns."

That phrase, "new living patterns," was clearly a euphemism for the rarity of domestic servants in post-World War II America. It probably also referred to a more casual approach to family life.

My eyes flew over the next few paragraphs as I excitedly read that if I agreed to attend the magazine would pay all my expenses, including a special allowance for babysitters "for those who need them."

Indeed, I would. Our daughter Jennifer had turned three in June. She would be easy. But her little brother, Chris, less than two, would be more of a handful. Luckily, their Uncle Jack and Aunt Nancy lived across the road from our farmhouse and were already well known to the children.

"What do you think?" I asked. "Could you help Jim with the kids while I'm gone?"

"Of course!" Nancy exclaimed, as Jack echoed her words almost in unison.

I'll be able to pay you," I hastened to add.

"That's swell," said Jack. "But what matters," he assured me, "is that you'll be able to go on this trip!"

"I'm so jealous," Nancy admitted. "But really," she added, smiling, "We will be glad to help out so YOU can go at least."

Discussing some of the logistics of child care that would be firmed up later, we continued to shake our heads in wonder over this almost unbelievable opportunity.

As I filled out the acceptance form, my thoughts looped from the thrill of imagining my first airplane flight to worrying about what on earth to wear. My wardrobe as a farmer's wife did not include any city clothes.

The tailored, dark blue dress that I sewed for myself proved to be appropriate when I met other delegates at the Shoreham, one of Washington's finest hotels.

Representing forty-five states, their average age was thirty-one. At twenty-eight, I was one of two women from Michigan. Three others and I were assigned to a large suite that represented unaccustomed luxury to me.

I had eagerly looked forward to seeing and hearing

the guest speaker for the opening banquet. The program listed her as Mrs. Eleanor Roosevelt. That designation was interesting, given that our delegate nametags and all printed materials gave only our husbands' names. Under *Mrs. James Gamble* on my badge, I penned "Judy"—an informal touch copied by others.

On a hotel postcard mailed home, I reported that the reception before the banquet lasted longer than scheduled because Mrs. Roosevelt was late. "As the champagne flowed for an extra hour, everyone got very mellow and much better acquainted," I wrote. "When we finally ate the thick rare roast beef, we needed it."

Mrs. Roosevelt spoke informally, at length, about her recent visit to Russia. My hotel postcard promised "details later," but I recall none today. What I do remember with pleasure is her unflagging cheer and seeming interest as she greeted each of us personally. As our hands met, I was reminded of how many she had to shake during her extensive public duties. Her fingers remained limp in mine. She clearly protected herself by not gripping. The "dead fish" handshake is often maligned, but for someone of prominence and fame, it was completely understandable—and sensible. There was nothing limp about her wide, familiar smile.

The delegates were said to represent a cross-section of America, reflecting varied levels of education, income, husbands' occupations, culture, family size and urban, suburban or rural homes. Looking now at photographs taken then, I am sorry but not surprised to note only two women of color.

Group discussions were held at tables for ten, each with

a facilitator and stenotypist. Delegates shared opinions on the functions of a home—not just the physical facility but aspects of what went on within the walls and what changes might promote greater ease and harmonious family life. About ninety-three percent of us owned our own homes.

The previous year, a federally-sponsored conference had given builders a clear idea of what women desired in housing styles. Our 1957 congress was focused more on interior design, furnishings, the function of spaces and the performance of appliances and household products. The aim was to demonstrate what consumers really wanted, not what manufacturers might think they ought to have.

There was no single question on which every one of the delegates agreed. But the majority opposed the enormous picture windows that builders then favored—the type that often just looked out onto a street or into someone else's picture window. But, the homemakers did prefer having the kitchen sink under a window, not on a blank wall.

They also favored more privacy inside the home.

"I wish my husband could have a den or home office in a pleasant part of the house, not just a corner of the basement," said the plump brunette at my table. Her remark is memorable because such a comfortable retreat is almost a given today, yet a separate "man cave" was quite uncommon in middle class homes back then.

"I suppose that might appeal to my husband, too," said the attractive redhead seated beside me. "But, first, I'd like a room of my own, like in that book by Virginia Wolff." We all nodded with understanding when she sighed, "I'm just expected to write letters or sew at the kitchen table."

A second bathroom was the home improvement most of the delegates craved, and compartmented spaces were favored over a large room with every bath fixture exposed.

In contrast, delegates liked the idea of returning to large kitchens as the hub of home life. The most popular design was a peninsula-like counter separating a U-shaped workspace from a family room so the cook could be included in conversations and supervise children. Common today, that concept became widely used by builders within a few years.

Opinions differed about separate dining rooms. East coast delegates were more apt to create formal, candlelight dinners than those of us from the Midwest or beyond. I remember a New Englander in an expensively tailored tweed suit who said, "It seems to me that informality is pushed and pushed until mealtime is no longer an event."

Agreeing, a stiffly-coiffed woman from Massachusetts said, "My husband and I believe that children learn manners better in a dining room."

Laughing, an outspoken California delegate countered, "I don't need a dining room to teach my kids manners. They can be taught in the family room or on the back patio just as well."

I remember one attractive brunette who always wore a hat, unlike most of us. She is also memorable for having said, rather sheepishly, "I hate cooking." It astonished me. I had completely succumbed to the societal expectation that a married woman produced delicious, nutritious, attractive meals daily and delighted in baking elaborate birthday cakes and six different kinds of Christmas cookies. How could any woman admit to hating that? As a farm wife, I was also expected to spend long sweaty hours doing seasonal canning.

The admission that I didn't enjoy it was shared only with my mother, who valiantly did what she could to help me every summer.

Almost all delegates agreed on a preference for natural materials in interior design—not wall coverings printed to resemble wood or brick or stone. One woman made it clear, "Public taste is much higher than manufacturers and retailers apparently think it is. I hate something that pretends to be something else."

The desire for more storage space was unanimous. "Larger bedroom closets," begged one delegate. "A separate linen closet," another chimed in.

"I would love to have a bigger garage," said a mother of four boys. "We need space for lawncare tools and outdoor furniture as well as the kids' bikes and sports equipment."

"I wish builders would offer built-ins for storing stuff like suitcases and Christmas decorations," said another homemaker.

And all of us wanted more electrical outlets in every room of the house.

Television was a comparatively new addition to family life for most of us that year. In the final report of the congress, the topic was not even listed in the index. It came up under discussion of what some people then called "rumpus rooms." Some of the mothers lamented the need to ration the amount of time their children watched TV. Others appreciated the educational programs. Adult viewing habits were not even discussed, except in the context of deciding where the set should be located. Nearly all the delegates agreed that, if possible, it should be kept out of the living room.

Home freezers were also relatively new in 1957. A Wisconsin

woman reported, "We are the only ones in our neighborhood that have one. Most of the guys go deer hunting in the fall, so I let my friends keep their venison in our freezer." Some families rented lockers in town, she said, but all longed for a freezer in their own kitchens.

Automatic washers and dryers were cited as appliances that provided the most convenience in women's servantless lives. One delegate said, "They could only be taken away over my dead body." As a mother who hung her first child's cloth diapers on outdoor clothes lines, I seconded that.

Manufacturers were paying close attention to the opinions that homemakers voiced during that week. Results were widely reported in all mass media. Descriptions of our two most-hated household chores actually led to solutions.

When I reported those to my granddaughter Stephanie, they did not surprise her. She had lived in enough old rental apartments to understand that the housewives declared how much they loathed the messy, smelly chore of keeping an oven clean. Although she still doesn't have such a convenience herself, she applauded the response of those late 1950's manufacturers who invented self-cleaning ovens.

And the most hated chore was, of course, ironing. All of the housewives who served as delegates to the first Women's Congress on Better Living later rejoiced that our complaints led to the development of adjustable ironing boards. And, hearing my tales, Stephanie then understood why I knew exactly when that happened. She and I feel sure that the concept of wash-n-wear fabrics was also inspired by that conference.

An optional tour of the White House was included in the congress. Since I had enjoyed that about ten years earlier, on a high school senior trip, I left the capital early Friday and took a train to New York City instead. McCall's' flexibility in making our travel arrangements allowed me to tack on a weekend in Manhattan with my beloved aunt, Lurry. She loved hearing every detail of my experiences as we feasted on exquisite Chinese food prepared by her friend Pearl Wang at her celebrated small restaurant.

On Saturday, Lurry and I joined Roy Bair, a friend of mine from Oberlin College. He had kept in touch across the years and the miles between our chosen lives. We three enjoyed lunch and several hours at the Museum of Modern Art before Roy treated me to dining and dancing at the fabled Roseland Ballroom.

That glittering evening capped the most memorable week of my youth. The all-expense-paid vacation—including my first airplane ride—was a delight in itself for a naïve young farm wife. The added feeling of having my personal opinions valued at an important nationwide event was a profound source of pride. After more than sixty years, I still have a bulging folder of yellowing newspaper clippings, articles from trade magazines, and the thick published report of conference results. After some judicious culling, the folder will go back on my closet shelf with a probably unrealistic hope that it will interest a *great*-grandchild.

馬

BOOK FIVE
CHERRYLAND NORTH

"The purpose of life,
after all, is to live it,
to taste experience to the utmost,
to reach out eagerly and without fear
for newer and richer experience."

– Eleanor Roosevelt

1

A Family Home

ALTHOUGH THE HOUSE we first rented in Traverse City was a cute contemporary, Jim and I were spoiled by the unique setting of our farm. We both hoped to find an affordable city home situated on an unusual lot.

While pregnant again, by choice, in 1960, we decided to buy a house on the older, more established, west side of town. We moved there in October and our second daughter was born February 13th, 1961. Named Cynthia and nicknamed Cyndi, she was a much-wanted little girl.

The house at 724 Sixth Street fit our desires and our budget. A smooth-flowing stream, called "Kids Creek" angled right across the side yard. A flat footbridge spanned the water and towering shade trees offered fat branches that could someday support a play-house.

From the two-car garage at the back, steep steps led up to the kitchen. A row of windows over the sink gave me the feeling of working in a tree-house of my own. For years we talked about building a deck on the garage roof. That never happened, but we completed many other projects inside and out.

As Jim and I celebrated our tenth wedding anniversary that next summer, we embarked on years of household remodeling.

The second story of our white frame house had two bedrooms, but the layout made it necessary to walk through the small one to get to the large one under the front eaves. Moreover, the stairs descended into the living room. Sleepy children had to stumble through adult conversations on their way through the dining room and on to the only bathroom. If we could just turn the stairs around, right in place, we thought, the kids would descend just steps away from the bathroom. Upstairs, the smaller room could be Cyndi's nursery, and we could divide the large space into two narrow, but separate, bedrooms for Jenny and Chris.

That's exactly what we did. An experienced carpenter, Carl Lempke, carried out the basic transformation. The timing is something I will never forget. On November 22, 1963, I was in the basement watching television while doing laundry and ironing. Cyndi, at two-and-a-half, divided her time between pestering patient "Mister Yemkee" (as she called him) and checking on me. To her astonishment, I suddenly dashed up two flights of stairs to weep with the carpenter as we digested the incredible news of President Kennedy's assassination. No more woodworking was done that day, as together in the basement, we absorbed the implications of the televised scenes.

Jim and I had been invited to have dinner with friends that evening. The hostess decided to go ahead with the gathering, feeling that we could all use the company to share and process the unimaginable news. We did draw support from one another.

As years went by, Jim's uncle, Kenney Turk, helped him remodel our basement into an attractive family room—with a small fireplace and a built-in "jazz couch" like the one in Pentwater. It served guests as well as for a day bed.

The kitchen went through two transformations—with paneling, paint and specialized carpeting. I had some creative fun installing a ceramic tile surround for the bathtub, while Jim relocated two doors and created storage space in the small hall.

Another winter he walled-over an unused door between our bedroom and the living room and replaced old-fashioned, well-nicked, wide woodwork with plain narrow boards darkly stained—creating a unique décor.

Jim and I found that our relationship was always at its best when we were working together on projects. Maybe a marriage needs more of a focus than gazing into each other's eyes. Ours did.

2

The Sixties

DURING A DECADE best known for the music of The
Beatles, America's incremental military enmeshment in
Viet Nam, long-haired hippies, anti-war protests and "open
marriage," I wore an apron over my bell-bottoms.

I found compatible friends by joining a Child Study
Club, the League of Women Voters and the Symphony
Women's Association. During the next few years, I
worked on geranium sales, chaired season ticket drives,
and launched a successful home tour—all to benefit the
Northwestern Michigan Symphony Orchestra. Tiring as all
this volunteering often felt, it fed my needy ego.

I also sought a venue for choral singing, which had
been a pleasure for me ever since high school. Early in our
marriage, Jim and I attended either a Congregational or
Methodist church– whichever had the best choir director.
In Traverse City that was Central Methodist, where Mel
Larimer began his outstanding career. I sang in that choir

until Jim and I helped to establish a Unitarian Universalist Fellowship. I maintained friendships with the Methodist singers Elsie Randall and Agnes Williams by performing with them in a large, all-city Community Chorale.

Our motive in forming the UU fellowship was to provide our growing children with some liberal religious education. We wanted to help them counteract what we considered myths that they were hearing from classmates. A school classmate once told Chris. "If I ever fell out of a tree, I wouldn't be hurt, because Jesus would catch me."

We had spotted a newspaper ad placed by two local women who wanted to raise their kids without dogma. Together with MaryAnn Force, Jan Park and others who answered the ad, we started meeting in September 1964. This timing coincided with efforts of the continental Unitarian Universalist Association to create liberal lay-led fellowships across the country, in communities that didn't have a UU church. In addition to UUA guidance, we were helped by downstate UU ministers.

Our fourth child, Scott Benjamin, who'd been born in August, snoozed on my shoulder during the organizational meetings.

The new Unitarian Universalist Fellowship of Grand Traverse initially met in classrooms and auditoriums at Northwestern Michigan College. Jim often taught Sunday school and we each held positions on the board, including president. I also wrote and "published" (on a Xerox machine) the weekly newsletter. And I learned to create worship services.

Unitarian Fellowships often fell into what has been jokingly called "The-Central-City-Sewer-System-Syndrome."

Programs featuring guest lectures on timely topics, followed by group discussion, were educational but hardly uplifting. The then UU district executive, the Rev. Bill Hammond, taught us how to create services that touched the heart as well as the head. I grew to love creating a format that, while not traditionally religious, included meaningful readings and good music as a setting for inspiring speakers—whether members or guests. I also assembled teams to create whole services around themes, and wrote a few myself. One popular service I staged was called "The Doctrine of N"—about an ancient Asian religion that was revealed to my father in 1931 on a mountaintop in China.

Bill Hammond also changed my life in another way. As district executive, he received newsletters from every church and fellowship in his territory, and he admired the one I wrote. In 1968, he asked me to edit a monthly statewide newsletter. Writing and laying out this four-page publication gave me skills I was able to apply to future paid employment.

...

My mother, Doré, retired from the staff at the University of Michigan and moved to Traverse City in 1967. We had always been emotionally close, but throughout my adult life we were physically separated nine months of the year. Living near each other again was sweet for both of us. She could walk from her small apartment to our house just four blocks away.

She kept me company while I ironed or cooked. In addition, she often stayed with her grandchildren while I attended some meeting or another. Many years later, from letters she wrote to her sister, I learned with chagrin that she often found this duty exhausting. But Doré never wanted to say no to me.

In the final years of the decade, I began hanging out at a head shop called Seventh House. Offering books, music and clothing as well as marijuana paraphernalia, the store was frequented by bearded, bead-wearing intellectuals, flower children and various dropouts from much of mainstream culture. One had been a founder of the UU Fellowship.

Phil Montague introduced me to the writings of the Beat Poets and Alan Watts and Krishnamurti. He also taught me to sail his twenty-one ft. twin-keel sailboat on the waters of Grand Traverse Bay and recharged the inner self that I had long ignored and even denied. I was Lara to his Zhivago. The boat was our dacha. Our love was equally star crossed.

My mother guessed at my double life but refused to discuss it. She reminded me that I had "made my bed" by having four children, and that I would have no way of supporting them if I sought a divorce.

"You've never even held a job," she threw at me.

True—then.

In 1969, after winter storms dumped heavy masses of snow on our city streets, Doré was severely injured. Thinking she was safe in stepping off a curb at a crosswalk, she didn't realize that wide piles of plowed snow had narrowed the traffic lanes. The pickup truck couldn't avoid hitting her.

She died two months later, about three months short of her 71st birthday. Much as I missed her, I knew that she had been ready to go for a long time. What I mourned was not just my loss but her lack of interest in living.

Both my parents were writers. Had Doré lived into the 1970s, she would have been proud to watch me go to work at the regional daily newspaper and applauded my later career.

3

Easter Sunday 1969

"Done," I said, feeling satisfied with the deep hem on Cyndy's new dress.

The pale blue cotton garment with puffed sleeves and a yoke of embroidered pink flowers, had been sensibly purchased a size large so she could grow into it. But it was too long to be cute. Because it was the only thing my eight-year-old daughter was willing to wear to church, nothing would do but that I take the time to turn up the hem. By the time I finished stitching, the clock revealed that holiday services would be starting within ten minutes.

Biting off the final thread, I slipped the precious raiment over the child's head and tied the wide sash at her back. As she danced off in delight, I called after her, "Please ask Daddy to come talk to me."

Her father, who had been helping our youngest child, four-year-old Scott Ben, to tie his shoes, was also urging our two older kids to hurry. "Huppy Ho," he would always say.

Jim was astonished to find me still in my robe and slippers, but understood my explanation.

"You go on ahead," I urged him. "Take the kids in the pickup and I'll drive over as soon as I get dressed." Luckily our Unitarian congregation was meeting in a rented chapel just a few blocks away. The family car was parked in the garage.

Earlier, to convince Cyndy of my intent to rush the alteration, I had carried pins, a sewing needle and blue thread, with her dress, to the back stairs. Separated from the kitchen by a half wall, they led down to the lower attached garage that opened to the driveway beside the house. Sitting on the bare wooden step, I heard the family pull away in the truck.

When I had completed my task, I slumped against the wall, my mind returning to thoughts that had preoccupied me for months. Increasingly despondent, I had dwelled on finding a way to end my life.

Back in January, on my 40th birthday, I had come to a firm decision that would determine the rest of my existence. I told my lover that I could not, would not, go away with him. Our affair had been transformative. Phil saw me as an individual, apart from the roles I had chosen. He nourished my soul, valued my mind, and taught the serious me to play! But, as much as I loved him, and had for two years, I just couldn't imagine myself living on a sailboat and combing beaches. And as much as Phil loved me, he couldn't imagine living with two young children. He felt that rearing his own children had killed romance with Irene. I had reluctantly assured him that I would let Jenny, 15, and Chris, 13, stay with Jim. But I wanted to have Cyndy and Scott with me. Impasse. Phil wouldn't take them. And I wouldn't leave them.

While my husband and Phil's wife knew of and tolerated our affair, neither of them knew how close we had come to "running away together."

When I refused to go, and Phil decided to move alone from Michigan to Florida, my world crumbled into a meaningless blur of pain. I couldn't face carrying on without him. A fragment of a poem I wrote then says,

I hear him say he has no need
for job, for money or for wife.
He'll only take his boat, some tools, his skills.
But does he know—he'd take my life?

That Easter morning, from my perch halfway up and halfway down the steep back stairway, I could see through the glass storm door at the bottom. As I gazed into the darkened garage, the unformed speculation that had occurred to me earlier slowly took shape.

I could start the engine, then lie down behind the car in the closed garage and breathe in the exhaust that would end my unhappy existence. I could see it: my body stretched out on the concrete, gradually relaxing as the blessed fumes brought longed-for oblivion.

For a few minutes, I succumbed to this vision—imagining release from the painful conflict between my quotidian reality and the romantic life I dreamed of.

But, as I lay on my side, facing the rear bumper of the car, another scene formed itself in my mind. I imagined Cyndy's horror when the family returned to find me dead. My husband and older kids would surely have been shocked and sad, but I assumed they would get over it. Scotty was so young, he might not even remember me. It was my little girl's reaction

I could envision. Would she blame herself? Would she think that asking me to hem her dress had caused me to commit suicide? Would she grow up with that shadow over her?

She was too young to comprehend that grown-ups had feelings, desires, or needs of their own. She might never forgive me for leaving her. She would surely be wounded, maybe permanently scarred by my action.

Lying there on the hard, cold surface, with such thoughts gradually overcoming my earlier resolve, I heard tires crunching on the gravel driveway. Scrambling to my feet, I rushed alongside the car and turned off the ignition. By the time Jim entered the garage, I was back in my earlier position on the steps leading up to the kitchen. If he noticed more exhaust fumes than usual, he didn't mention it. I arranged my features as he looked up at me.

"When you didn't come along soon, I wondered if you were all right," he said. "I figured I'd better come back and see…"

"I'm OK," I answered. "Just lazy. I hope the kids are all having fun on the Easter egg hunt."

"Okay…Oh yes…they're so excited. Great fun. I left Peg in charge. So I'll head back now…" he called over his shoulder as he jogged off toward the truck to fetch our children.

I'm sure he had no inkling of what I had felt or tried to do.

Neither of us ever mentioned my absence from the holiday festivities.

Reflecting today on the woman I was then, I am well aware of the irony. I had refused to abandon my young daughter and her little brother to sail off into the sunset with my lover. Yet, on that Easter Sunday, I had been set on abandoning them through death.

That was the first time love of Cyndy saved my life.

4

The Record-Eagle

"WHEN ARE YOU GOING to come work for us?" asked the editor of the regional daily newspaper.

Bill Smith never failed to pose this question whenever I submitted another feature story on behalf of the League of Women Voters. My articles on welfare reform had become popular among readers of the *Traverse City Record-Eagle*, and the editor heard kudos for my writing.

My answer was always, "When my kids are in school all day."

While our four children were small, Jim and I just assumed that he would be the breadwinner and my job was to be homemaker and mother. It was the unspoken pattern followed by most families in those days.

We also filled many hours with volunteer work for our Unitarian Universalist Fellowship, and I edited a statewide newsletter for the UU District. The Symphony Women's Association and the League of Women Voters' activities were rewarding.

In 1970, following the League's study of welfare reform, the board asked me to write the informational series for the paper. Even as I basked in praise for the results, I gave little thought to employment. Even after Scott Ben, our youngest, entered first grade, I procrastinated. In the summertime, the family loved spending as much time as possible in Pentwater.

The resort village that had been my mother's vacation refuge nestled on the shore of Lake Michigan a hundred miles south of Traverse City. After Doré's death in 1969, I inherited the house. The kids and I stayed there most of July and August. Jim usually managed three-day weekends, to share in long, mellow hours on the beach.

But, by early 1972 I yearned for greater personal fulfillment. So, I went back to the *Record-Eagle* newsroom to see Bill Smith.

"Remember when you asked if I could come work for you?" I asked, after accepting the chair across from him at his desk.

"Sure I do," answered the stocky, grey-haired newsman.

"Well, I'm ready now, if you still want me on the staff." Nervously fearing rejection, I held my breath.

To my relief, Bill quickly said, "I would love to hire you. But…"

My worry returned.

…the only job open right now is tape girl," he continued.

What's that?" I questioned the word "girl," since I had just observed my 43rd birthday.

Smiling, Bill explained. The job had previously been held by very young women. The simple, entry-level task required someone to take the inch-wide punched paper strips, called tapes, that ticked in from the wire services—Associated Press and UPI—and match them with printed teletype versions of each story, clip them together and hang them on appropriate hooks. From the hooks, Managing Editor Frank Watson selected his choices for the day's paper, to be augmented by local news.

It would be quite a few years before everything would be done by computer. In the 1970s, every line of type appearing on a newspaper page was set by hand with tiny lead letters in slotted rows. Each full sheet laid out in this "hot lead" method would be inked repeatedly before being covered by newsprint unrolling from enormous spools. Huge machines pressed the paper onto the type and peeled it off again to create each page of the newspaper. The odor of that ink still lingers in my senses. The steamy, noisy printing plant looked and sounded just as it appears in old movies. "Hot off the presses" was daily routine.

No one had a personal computer. A reporter typed each story on a typewriter, turned it in to Frank, who edited it in pencil and sometimes handed it back to be retyped before it was passed along to one of those typesetters on deadline! Thinking back on those days, I wonder if anyone in the editorial department even knew of computers outside of the room-sized behemoths invented for industry or the corporate world.

After Bill Smith described the work to me that day in his office, I asked, "If I came on as tape girl, would I be able to do any writing?"

"Absolutely," Bill responded. "If you can manage to do some feature stories after your tape girl duties, I would be glad to publish them."

On that basis, I took the job and began in February.

Reflecting today on how life changed for me from then on, it seems ironic that my volunteer work led to employment. My mother had never understood what she called my "civic matron do-gooder" activities, and she once chided me about never having held a "real job." Now, a real job had resulted from talents I'd honed without pay. Doré would have been proud if she'd lived to see what I went on to achieve in later years.

After starting at the *Record-Eagle*, I often stayed on into the evening to type my features. But soon my byline was appearing regularly. Whenever Jim was also working late, I counted on Jenny, seventeen, and Chris, fifteen, to supervise their two younger siblings. They were already dependable household helpers and sitters for Cyndy and Scott. Without that backup, I probably could not have taken on an outside job.

Within a few months, I was relieved of hanging teletype tapes and assigned to the local entertainment beat. Each Friday, a full page called "Fun 'n' Stuff" detailed all the regional performances scheduled for the coming week. My job required me not only to list the movies, plays and concerts, but call all the lounges and bars in the area to find out what musicians would be appearing there on weekends. Most newspaper readers never think about who gathers that information. I can attest that it often takes repeated phone calls. Not exactly fun!

Meanwhile, my human-interest features were increasingly well-received. In a series called "The Many Faces of Eve," I profiled area women who had succeeded in roles previously considered masculine terrain. One was an attorney who wanted readers to know, "I never won a case because I'm a woman. And I never lost a case because I'm a woman."

A local female pilot who had set a speed record in winning the longest trans-continental "Powder Puff Derby" was the subject of another popular feature. She was one of thirteen American women to undergo astronaut testing and served on President Nixon's Aviation Advisory Board.

The following year, when the women's editor took her vacation, I was asked to fill in. The elegant, white-haired Catherine "Katie" Carroll was entitled to a month off by then—having edited the so-called society section for *40 years*!! So, her absence gave me a chance to prove myself. The following year, when Katie retired, I was moved into the job and given a rare opportunity.

To some extent at least, the newspaper was ready to move with the times. In early 1974, it was decided that the old "Women's World" section should be updated. I was given the responsibility of creating a new section which would reflect the interests of 1970s women. They wanted to read about more than just social events, weddings, engagements, food and fashion. After broadly researching what was being done at big city dailies, I tackled the assignment with enormous pride and pleasure.

I called the new section "Spectrum." I loved choosing stimulating wire service stories and interviewing interesting local subjects for features. Most readers were enthusiastic about the changes, but acceptance was not universal. I soon learned that Bill Smith had a broader agenda. He had long harbored pet peeves about the women's pages, and he expected *me* to eliminate them.

The toughest task was telling the garden clubs, church guilds and various ladies auxiliaries that the *Record-Eagle* would no longer publish detailed reports of their meetings—reports that amounted to full minutes of their activities including names of all the women who decorated the hall, created handmade favors, poured the tea, passed the pastries and presided over the "tastefully appointed" tea tables.

Mothers of brides could be heard complaining throughout the newsroom when I cut out detailed descriptions of the bride's gown—the heart-shaped neckline edged with Chantilly lace, the princess cut dropped waist, the gossamer veil held by a crown of lilies-of-the-valley, and the six-foot-long peau-de-soie train—not to mention eliminating the styling and color of each bridesmaid's dress, the type and hue of each flower surrounded by baby's breath in every bouquet, the adorable decorations atop a three-tiered cake and the stunning floral arrangements.

Some mothers pleaded.

Some threatened.

Some sobbed.

I ducked—behind a shiny shield of "policy."

A few irate women never spoke to me on the street again. But other readers rejoiced. And fan mail poured in.

I did include a food feature now and then, with some clipable recipes, but "Spectrum" always led with a weighty feature about a clever, talented, dedicated local woman who was achieving major progress in the community—and often in the state and nation.

My name and face, in a thumbnail photo, appeared on

the section's leading page every day, so I worked long hours to make sure each issue was as fine as possible. Longer hours than others might have, I feel sure, because my old demon Perfectionism caused me to think and rethink the placement of every story as I created a "dummy" mock-up of each page. Taking the word count of each article, I had to estimate how many column inches it would require, and whether it deserved a six-column headline (out of the total of eight) or only a two or three. All the text on the mock page had to fit around the commercial advertisements that were the paper's bread and butter.

Moreover, I often assigned myself a local interview and feature story. It was worth the extra time, because I loved spotlighting otherwise unknown people who deserved recognition for significant accomplishments. A two-part feature on Special Education was widely appreciated by teachers and by parents of handicapped children.

One favorite feature began, "In the 71st year of her life, hair white sifted, Ethel Gray Seese has seen publication of a volume of her collected poems. The author has been sorting treasured bits from the chaff of life for many years, and her poetry has appeared in anthologies and magazines. But this is the first time a selection of her poems has been winnowed in one array. The reader reaps."

This Kentucky native who'd retired to a tiny Northern Michigan village told me why she never tried to earn a college degree. "Life's too short to work on assignments." But she found that she could "take wild, flaming words and shape them into candlelight." Indeed.

I had been given a dream job, and for two years working

at *The Record-Eagle* was more fulfilling than I could have imagined. Then late one afternoon, the editors and advertising directors were summoned to an unusual five o'clock meeting in the publisher's office.

"What's up?" we all wondered. The last thing we expected was what we heard.

The *Traverse City Record-Eagle* had been a family-owned newspaper for more than eighty years. Publisher Robert Batdorff had succeeded his father and grandfather at running the Northern Michigan daily. Now, at the height of their success, the family had decided to sell the paper.

"We received an offer that we just couldn't refuse," Bob explained. "The Ottaway Newspaper chain, based in Middleport, New York, will be taking over in 30 days...."

Seeing our astonishment, he assured us, "All your jobs are secure. No changes in personnel are planned."

Bill Smith, however, was shrewd enough to see what was coming. He decided it was time to retire. When the head honchos at the Ottaway Company selected his replacement, they decided to bring in a man already trained by them, who was currently heading another newspaper in their chain.

That feisty Easterner became the second editor to change my life.

5

On a Darkling Beach

AROUND THE TIME I went to work at *the Record-Eagle*, Traverse City's daily newspaper, our two teenagers, Jenny and Chris, took after-school jobs. In the summer of 1972, their hours were expanded and usually included weekends. Knowing that we would no longer be able to spend much family time in Pentwater, Jim and I decided to rent out the house there during the tourist season. The income would help to pay the taxes and maintenance. The motive was worthy, but implementation was a challenge.

First, we had to remove all Doré's Chinese scroll paintings and treasures. That was a given. It wasn't fun to strip the place of its familiar look, but necessary. Then we had to find reliable renters—to take the house for at least a week, preferably two or more. Little did we dream that people who answered ads on church bulletin boards could be such slobs.

Between renters, Jim and I drove the hundred miles to take sheets and towels to the Laundromat and clean the premises. We spent long hours every weekend scrubbing and mopping before the next group arrived. These people had good references. Yet, once, when we entered in their wake, the place looked and smelled like a roadhouse bar on New Year's Day. The disappointment was discouraging. And because we never did attract long-term renters, we never had a leisurely weekend for ourselves.

So, as the following summer of 1973 approached, we forced ourselves to look at alternatives. "Now that we can't enjoy Pentwater summers ourselves, I really think we ought to sell the house," Jim said with some hesitation, anticipating my reaction.

"Oh, I hate to think of doing that," I lamented, not for the first time. "I dream of the day when the kids will have kids of their own and we can all gather there for family reunions..."

"I've thought about that, too. But we can't just let it sit empty, and we can't afford to hire someone else to clean the house between renters, and...."

"I know," I sighed, stopping him from repeating reasons we'd been over so often. "You were a good sport to try the rentals as a way of keeping the house. And I sure admit that plan didn't work. Let me think about it...." Although brokenhearted, I finally had to acknowledge that Jim was right. The house was dearer to me, because I had spent my childhood summers there and it had been my mother's beloved refuge. But Jim had devoted a lot of time and attention to the maintenance while our children were small and spent time there with their grand-mother. He loved it, too. Yet keeping it now for some fairytale future didn't make sense. To decide based on wishful thinking would be sentimental folly.

"OK," I finally told him. "I'll call a Realtor. But it matters a lot to me that we sell to someone who will love the house just as much as we have—other summer resorters, not just a local landlord who will modernize it or neglect it."

Our first offer was from a Big Oil company who would use it to house temporary rig workers who were pouring into the village after new area wells proved lucrative. "*No way!*" I declared.

Luckily, the daughter of the family that lived across the street was thrilled to learn that our house was on the market and offered to buy it at a fair price. A few years younger than I was, Martha knew me only by sight. But she had spent her youthful summers on that street, knew that our parents had been friends, and loved the idea of buying a house right opposite her folks'.

Jim and I spent much of June 1973 moving family memorabilia to Traverse City and prepping the Pentwater house. Martha bought all the beds and other basic cottage-style furnishings, so they could be left in place. The closing was held Saturday, July 14th, with an agreement that we could stay over until Sunday afternoon.

We had been invited to a farewell Sunday brunch at Jim's uncle's cottage on the North Beach dunes. After that, we planned to drive to the nearby town of Hart, to say goodbye to his brother Jack Gamble and wife Nancy. The day was unusually hot and muggy. Because the noon meal ran late, our younger children, Cyndy, 12, and Scott, 8, had missed a second swim.

Sticky with sweat, they begged to be let off at the state park beach, instead of having to endure the car ride to Hart and obligatory family visit. Chris, 17, wanted to see Jack and Nancy. He had worked hard cleaning house and loading furniture, so we said he could come with us—permission followed by howls from the back of the station wagon!

"Oh, *please* let us stay on the beach," wailed Cyndy. "I'm *so* hot! We just want to get into the water. We promise we'll stay right on the edge of the sand or in the shallow water, don't we Molly?"

Cyndy's 13-year-old friend Molly Spaulding had come along from Traverse City for the weekend. It seemed unfair to keep her away from Lake Michigan, where cool waves promised relief from the oppressive heat.

As Jim and I dithered, the kids kept up their appeal.

"We promise not to go out deep, don't we Scott?" Cyndy said, enlisting her usual accomplice.

"Uh huh," Scott vowed. "*Promise!*"

So we dropped them off. When Jim helped lug towels and toys to the water's edge, he noticed that the surf was higher than it had been earlier. Our children had been warned all their lives about the undertow from powerful waves. Once more the two girls pledged to be careful, so he came back to the car and we drove off.

...

When the phone rang at Jack and Nancy's house, a state park employee told us that we had better come back to the Pentwater beach, because, "Your son is lost."

Whether that young man didn't understand what Cyndy was telling him, or whether he was trying to cushion a blow, he did not convey the truth. And he did not put our daughter on the phone. So we drove north with only minor anxiety, hoping Scott would be found by the time we arrived.

"Scott is probably teasing the girls by hiding somewhere," Jim said.

"Yeah. He's probably up in one of the cubbyholes in the dunes," I guessed.

As we drove slowly past the guard booth at the park entrance, the uniformed man on duty called out to us, "They're afraid that your son drowned. A bunch of people are out there looking for him..."

Drowned?! I could feel my heart pounding as I tried to absorb that possibility. Before our car was fully parked, Chris sprang out of the back door and dashed down across the sand. Already wearing his swim suit, he shucked off his shoes and plunged in to join a line of volunteers in deep water. Hands holding hands, men and women had formed a human chain, moving slowly, ever-so-slowly, fighting waves as they scanned the area for his beloved little brother.

Jim and I hurried down to where Cyndy and Molly sat shivering on the sand. There, little by little, we learned what they had been through.

Yes, our kids had been repeatedly warned about undertow, but youngsters feel invincible. And they want to have fun. The girls yearned to swim out to the sandbar, where other kids were jumping the crashing breakers with squealing delight. Knowing they could not leave Scotty alone, they reluctantly agreed to pull him along. The water was soon over his head.

"Scott got tired and started for shore, but called for help on his way in," Cyndy said. "I went to him and grabbed his hand. I knew enough to stay out of the undertow, so we both swam on our backs, holding hands heading back out to the sandbar so we could stand up and rest."

What she didn't know is that they were drifting towards the pier, and that the undertow near it had wiped out the sandbar. When Scott tried to put his feet down to touch bottom, the powerful waves tore his hand from Cyndy's grasp.

Scott disappeared.

Shocked and afraid, the two girls struggled back toward shore. Without the help of two twentyish young women, they, too, might have gone under.

After we hugged them with deep gratitude that they were safe, and thanked the strangers who rescued them, we assured our daughter that we did not blame her for what happened. Cyndy later said that the words of a neighbor were a blessing. "Whatever you remember about this night," Mary Ann Bates told her, "remember that it was not your fault."

As friends expressed their shock and sorrow, I struggled to accept reality. How could Scott possibly be gone? Just one month before his ninth birthday. The ache made it difficult to breathe. *Surely they will find him and he'll be all right,* I thought.

Then the Coast Guard showed up. A kind officer led Jim and me to a bench on higher ground, where we answered his questions. Out on the lake we saw small Coast Guard cutters running slowly in deep water, beyond the line of human searchers. Perhaps his explanation shouldn't have shocked me, but it did. "By now," he said, "We are just looking for a body."

Numbness took me over. No tears flowed. At that time in my life, I had no idea how to acknowledge feelings. This "survival mechanism" served me well—then. Only years later did I learn to label and express emotions.

Jim, who was equally adept at walling off his feelings, needed to do something. He decided to go back to our house, where he could make a long distance call to our elder daughter Jenny, before she heard from someone listening to radio or television news. She had stayed alone in Traverse City that weekend because she had to work at her waitressing job. Hearing of the tragic accident on the telephone was a terrible shock. She adored her baby brother. Jenny understood her dad's need to call her, but apparently his message seemed abrupt. She later said she wished the blow had been softened, somehow. Luckily, a good friend could come over afterwards, to spend the night with her.

Jim also called Kathy Spaulding, mother of Cyndy's friend Molly. She was very understanding and supportive. And he contacted someone at *The Record-Eagle*, to tell them I wouldn't be in for work on Monday. The new owners of our Pentwater house were among the neighbors who sheltered our little survivors on the beach. They assured us we could sleep there another night.

Knowing that Cyndy was safe with those friends, wrapped warmly in their beach blankets, I stayed on the bench high above. When the human chain of volunteers had to give up its fruitless search, Chris joined his little sister. She remembers how they sat together in the group, hugging their own knees.

As dusk deepened into darkness, a stranger asked to share my bench. I had wanted solitary space, but nodded, trusting he would not intrude. I watched the boats and wished, aloud, on the first bright star.

"That's Venus," said my new companion. "Look! The Big

Dipper is emerging!"

Mutely, I stared past his outstretched finger, willing my mind to absorb his words.

"In fact, the Dipper is just the brightest part of a bear," he genially informed me. "The handle is the tail of Ursa Major— the Great Bear to the Greeks and Iroquois alike... Did you know that in England the Dipper is called The Plough? And in mediaeval times those stars were seen as a wagon hitched to a horse. The first astronomers were farmers. By noting the movement of imagined constellations, they could tell when to hunt and sow and reap."

To every thing there is a season... I mused silently.

As he named the Dipper's seven lettered stars, my hands rose to my wind-tossed hair. Then tying a blue bandana 'round my head, I concentrated on the boats....

"Cassiopeia is my favorite constellation," my bench mate told me, as I tuned in again. "Look there to the north. It's faint, but see? It forms a W."

For Weeping? I wondered to myself.

The man's soft voice was soothing, but my thoughts spun away from his. I wondered why the use of stars transcended their timeless splendor. For eons those radiant clusters had blazed across vast voids of inky space. Why do sailors set a course by them?

*The certainty of stars can comfort, reassure...*I told myself. *When hope exists.*

Yet, I remembered, the Dipper's stars are separating slowly. They will not hold the pattern we expect. And stars whose beauty we admire today, disintegrated hundreds of light years before. As we "wish our wish come true" upon their brilliance, I thought, they are oblivious to petty human woes. They're named for ancient gods, somehow symbolic of indifference to mere mortals' fears.

Star light. Star bright. Take this cup from me tonight.

Noticing my wavering attention, the sociable stranger quieted, then observed my gaze and lowered his to follow—to the boats—to the power boats' measured move-ments, back—and—forth—their arcing searchlights probing cold black waters, still choppy in the dying wind.

"I think they're looking for a body," said the amateur astronomer. "I heard that a little boy had drowned."

"Yes," I managed to confirm. "My son."

...

When Jim returned to pick me up, and shepherded Cyndy, Molly and Chris into the car as well, we drove silently back to the old house, which was no longer ours. No longer adorned by my mother's pictures, flower-filled vases or Asian artifacts, it lacked any cozy familiarity, but was still a welcome refuge. Finally, long after midnight, Jim and I lay wrapped around each other in one single-width bed and, at last, wept.

6

The Morning Glory

THE FOLLOWING MORNING, the star-gazing stranger was among the curious on-lookers at the Pentwater Lake Marina. Coast Guard personnel had found Scott's body under the pier at the end of the long channel that connects Lake Michigan with the inland lake. We were told that a cutter would bring "it" to the marina where we could claim our child.

The anguish in the eyes of my previous evening's companion moved me to walk over to him. "Thank you," I said.

"Oh gosh...if I had known...I am SO sorry about your son...."

"Of course," I assured him. "It's okay, really. I needed the diversion right then. Thanks...." I walked back to the wall by the water.

Barbara Gwillim, a cousin of Jim's, warned me that Scotty would not look like himself when his body was turned over to us. "He will be all bloated and pasty white," she declared. "You don't want to see that and remember him that way."

As she blocked my way, Barbara took from my hands an antique cotton quilt that we had brought to the marina. With strong suntanned legs in short white shorts, she jumped down into the power boat, quickly wrapped our son and lifted him up to his daddy's waiting arms.

Reverently, Jim placed his precious burden into a narrow, unadorned cedar chest in the back of our station wagon. This plain family heirloom would suffice as a comforting coffin.

We had previously learned from a friend that Michigan law allows individuals to deliver a body to a crematory. No licensed undertaker is required. Our friend had not only transported his wife's body, he even built her coffin as she lay dying of cancer.

A coroner met the Coast Guard officials at the marina and gave us a signed death certificate. If he disapproved of our plans, he did not voice it. Then, leaving Cyndy and Molly with Barbara, Jim and I drove to Grand Rapids. Friends told me later that some of the muted muttering at the marina had been critical of us. Had we heard it, we would not have been deterred. We believed that our farewell to Scott was gentler and more loving than turning him over to a mortician.

We spoke little on the drive—both emotionally numb. It wasn't disbelief. It was a shared silence as we struggled to accept the unimaginable reality of our loss. I had learned years earlier that it is pointless to cry "Why me?!" The better question, I think, is "Why *not* me?" None of us is spared a share of life's tragedies.

Jim was naturally curious about the stranger I'd spoken with at the marina.

"I don't know who he is," I explained, describing the

connection. "Probably a boater." It hadn't seemed necessary to ask his name. We never saw him again, but I'll never forget his star-gazing presence the night Scott drowned.

We'd called ahead. The crematory employees were kind. Soon it was over.

On the drive north again, I was struck by regret. How I wished that I had climbed into the back of the station wagon, opened the cedar chest and cradled my little boy in my arms. I wish I'd known then what I later learned from our elder son. Chris had been among the helpers at the end of the pier when Scott's body was found. "He just looked asleep," Chris told us that night. "He wasn't puffy or discolored or anything like that."

How I wished I'd held Scotty one more time. I still do.

What a cruel irony it was that two painful passages occurred on the same weekend. I can never forget when we sold the Pentwater house, because it was the day before our beloved son drowned. Although not of the same magnitude, the losses are indelibly linked.

When we returned to Traverse City, I telephoned Frank Gentile, a family friend who was a Unitarian Universalist minister in Southfield, Michigan. We had become close when he conducted some personal growth workshops, called T (for training) Groups, for a dozen of us from our congregation and the Midland Fellowship. In fact, one of the weekend-long sessions had been held in our Pentwater house.

After describing our tragedy, I asked Frank if he could come to conduct a memorial service.

"I'll come," he answered. "But not just to conduct a service. That is something we will create together. I will come because I must be with you."

We set the date and time for Friday, early evening. The Ludington UU Fellowship offered to host the service in its attractive small white-framed building. The location, not far for Gamble family members and friends who would come north from Hart and Pentwater, was still convenient for those who might drive south from Traverse City. With robot-like efficiency, I wrote an obituary and designed invitations.

All the modeling of my childhood and adolescence had been that loss is simply a part of life. I believed that my role was to demonstrate that life went on. Barely acknowledging the stabbing dimensions of my own heartbreak, even to myself, I went back to work at the newspaper office on Tuesday morning.

It was my first full-time job. I assumed I was expected to show up. No one had ever told me about something called "bereavement leave." It had never come up. I put in a few hours at my desk before my shocked *Record-Eagle* colleagues sent me home.

Tuesday evening and Wednesday we welcomed callers. While aching with guilt over not protecting my child from death, I comforted the friends who came to comfort me. A year or so later, a good friend confided that she had been totally mystified by my dry-eyed behavior. "It was as if you didn't care that your child had died," she said. Hearing her words, my initial urge was to protest and explain, but I quickly realized that she had wanted me to cry on her shoulder. She'd needed to be needed.

I also believed that I must not cry in front of my other three children, for fear that they would think that *they* were less important to me than the one we lost. Years later, Jenny told me that what she internalized was that if I didn't cry over Scott, how would I feel if *she* died?

When Frank arrived on Thursday, he sat the family down and together we created a beautiful celebration of Scott's brief life. My previous experience crafting UU Sunday services helped me understand his suggestions about weaving together words and music.

Jenny and two friends formed a trio to sing "Little Boy Blue," the poignant musical setting of Eugene Fields' poem. Cyndy shared personal memories of her little brother and Chris read a poem by A.A. Milne. Recorded music included Barbra Streisand's "Where is the Wonder?" and "The Dance of the Sugarplum Fairy" from "The Nutcracker Suite." Scott used to stretch out on the floor in front of our old phonograph cabinet to listen to that and other marches from the Tchaikovsky classic. Jim participated in planning the service but preferred not to speak.

Frank Gentile's message was based on lines from *The Little Prince* by Antoine de Saint Exupéry. "Tell me what you have done for your rose," the boy in the story was asked. After describing his careful tending of the flower, the little prince was told, "It is the time you have wasted for your rose that makes your rose so important."

When the floor was opened to anyone who wanted to speak, many heartwarming memories were shared about a delightful little boy—Scott's pride in handling the tiller of Phil's sailboat; Scott and his best friend Mark Nelson, at bath time, wrapping themselves in the shower curtain and pretending to be a TV spot for a cleaning product called "Janitor in a Drum."

At the end, I spoke from my front row seat and told of the lullabies that I sang to Scott as I tucked him in at night. I said that I wanted to close our service as if I were perched on the edge of his bed to bid him a sweet sleep. Seated, and unaccompanied, I sang, "Sweetest little fellow anybody knows, don't know what to call him, but he's mighty lak a rose."

After a few moments I stood and said, "Please join us now for some refreshments. Scotty always liked that part of any gathering the best." Responsive chuckles told me that the light invitation was a welcome touch, breaking the heaviness everyone felt.

For our family and friends, the service was deeply meaningful and healing. Only Jim's stepmother felt cheated. She needed reassurance that Scotty was in Heaven with Jesus. That was not something we could provide, but we understood her underlying fear. If that sweet child wasn't safe in the arms of the Lord, what did that foretell for her?

I do not believe in heaven, hell or any other sort of afterlife. I believe that our human existence on this earth is all we get. Yet, I had no idea, that summer, what a high price I would pay for my stoicism after such a loss.

Still, death happens even to the young. We were blessed to have Scott Benjamin Gamble in our lives for nearly nine years.

As a Zen poet wrote,

The morning glory
which blooms for an hour
differs not at heart from the giant pine
that lives for a thousand years.

7

"This is the Editor Speaking!"

"GET OUT THERE and dig up the dirt," bellowed our new editor.

Shock lifted the reporters' eyebrows as they took in their new reality. During the 60 years that the Batdorff family owned the *Traverse City Record-Eagle*, their values of decency and respectability dictated what was fit to print. Readers had long observed that the foibles of rich men's sons were rarely published in the daily news-paper. They also noticed that attention was paid to trivial activities of certain prominent citizens. This was to change—radically— but no one could have foreseen it when I joined the staff in 1972.

Two years later, when the Batdorffs sold the paper to the Ottaway Company, the chain immediately appointed a new editor. Lee Lapensohn was a feisty, thirty-something Easterner with something to prove. The smarmy charm that he initially spread around had a certain appeal. But the slick veneer soon cracked to reveal his true character.

Asserting his full 5 ft. 6 inches of height, and scowling from under heavy black brows, our compact new editor frenetically paced the newsroom like Napoleon reviewing the troops. Black-rimmed glasses fronted squinched dark eyes as he took it upon himself to transform our regional paper.

In that post-Watergate era, the new journalistic emphasis nationwide was on investigative reporting, and Lee was determined to turn the *Traverse City Record-Eagle* into the next *Washington Post*. He ordered all the general assignment reporters to emulate Woodward and Bernstein. Gone were the days of special treatment for the old guard of the community. If anything, they made a favored target for Lee's venomous pursuit.

Once, when a staff photographer refused to click away at a mother who had just witnessed her son run over by a car, the editor thundered, "You bleeding sissy! Don't ever miss such an ideal human interest shot again!"

Lee was way ahead of his time in appealing to the lowest common denominator of readers. The more sickening the better. I will never forget the staff meeting at which Lee gave us all a dressing down for our tender-hearted reluctance to smear.

"I not only want to know whose hand is in who else's pocket," he yelled. "I want to know who pees in the gutter!"

To call his treatment of the staff unkind is to minimize the way he terrorized us. It soon became apparent that one of Lee's immediate goals was to replace mature employees with a younger generation of reporters more in tune with his way of thinking. Even he knew that he couldn't just fire the experienced journalists, so he used deviously clever methods of getting what he wanted.

First he took sweet fifty-something Marie Averill off the soft features she'd been writing for years and assigned her to the police beat! Valiantly, Marie followed his orders to stop by the city police station every morning on her way to work, to pick up the daily blotter report. When she handed the report to Lee, he would fire questions at her: "What is this person accused of? Why was this arrest made? How soon did the police arrive at the scene?" As Marie tearfully explained that the desk sergeant would not give her that information, Lee sighed loudly with feigned exasperation, bounded over to his desk, dialed the station and insisted on speaking to the chief of police.

"This is the editor speaking!" he yelled into the phone, demanding an answer to his questions, all the while glaring at poor Marie, who knew she had to face another inquisition when she wrote up the story. After about six months of this, Marie decided that she and her husband David could get along on his salary as a columnist, and she resigned. Lee never messed with David.

Women were his preferred target, and I was next. The tactic he used with me was equally clever. First he flattered me on my sharp mind. Then he maintained that my writing was too good to be relegated to Spectrum, the section I edited, which he insisted on calling the women's pages. He assigned me to attend evening meetings of community groups that had to be covered for the next day's paper. I generally worked through the supper hour to design the lay-out for Spectrum before heading off to the meetings and returned to the newsroom at 11 p.m. to finish that job and to write the story on the Water Resources Commission or the Gas and Oil Advisory Board.

The ease with which today's editors manipulate computer images of what they want on a newspaper page was inconceivable then. On a mock page of newsprint, I had to pencil instructions for the width and length of each column, designate the position for each photo, and make educated guesses about how much of a given story would make it into type. Plagued as I was by self-defeating perfectionism, each "dummy" page layout took me what I now acknowledge was an unrealistic amount of time to complete. I sometimes rubbed holes into the paper with repeated erasures.

Exhaustion defined my days. Whenever I tried to talk to Lee Lapensohn about my workload, he would switch subjects or his condescending dismissal of my concerns reduced me to tears. It's embarrassing, today, to reflect on how easily I cried back then. When women felt powerless to defend ourselves or express real feelings, we wept.

Lee's other tactic was to divert me by asking my valued opinion about some new scheme of his that he could trust only *me* to appreciate. Sometimes he would confide in me about the pressures he felt in his own life. I would end up apologizing for bothering him and choke down my own needs and emotions.

As months of this treatment went by, Lee piled on the assignments, saying, "I'm counting on you, Judy. No one else could do this half as well."

In response to my mounting frustration, he came up with the thoughtful idea of having my assistant, Vi Eitner, decide what stories would go into the Spectrum section and to "dummy" the pages each day. This did free me to get home to my family more evenings, because I could type news stories at home after the children went to bed. But it worried me, because Vi took the path of least resistance by plugging in UPI or AP wire stories, gave up local features, and took no particular pains with layout. So, although my name and thumbnail photo appeared on the Spectrum lead page every day, the section no longer reflected my standards. As fatigue was compounded by frustration, my despair deepened.

One Sunday night, depressed and exhausted, I swallowed the contents of a bottle of Valium. Discovered by my husband, who called a doctor, I was forced to vomit until out of danger. I didn't want to die. The tranquilizer wouldn't have killed me. I just wanted to sleep so long that I would never have to go back to that newspaper office.

I never did.

Following my resignation, I received a tidy check representing a month's salary and accumulated sick leave. Although Lee's subsequent decision didn't surprise me, I hated hearing that Vi Eitner was promoted into my job. But, my relief was stronger than regret about the diminished quality of "Spectrum."

Although I rarely saw Lee Lapensohn again, my connection with that cunning tormentor did not end there. A local judge brought a law suit against the *Traverse City Record-Eagle* and its editor for deliberate defamation of character. "Finally!" we all thought, "Somebody in town has the guts to take on that banty emperor who has given journalism such a bad name."

I had been on staff when the original story hit the streets. I knew full well that Lee had a vendetta against that judge. He told us so. He made no secret of his plan to dig up all the dirt he could, and to print innuendoes about half truths. Although I bore no ill will against the newspaper or my friends who still worked there, I knew that I could say what they could not. I offered to testify against the editor.

By the time the case came to court in 1982, I was living in New Jersey, but I agreed to fly back to Michigan to give a deposition. I recounted my recollections about staff meetings at the *Record-Eagle*, and particularly that infamous quotation about "who pees in the gutter." My testimony established Lee's news-gathering style, but others showed he did it to sell newspapers, not out of malice toward the plaintiff. Demonstration of malice was needed for proof of libel. So, the paper won. But Lee Lapensohn was assigned to another Ottaway newspaper. And a few years later, when he was just in his early 40s, a third heart attack took his life.

In one of those closed-door conferences, back when I danced to Lee's tune, he revealed that he was the only son of an obsessively demanding father. Perhaps it is unsurprising that his "type A" personality developed as it did. Looking back, I feel a little bit sorry for Lee. But my association with him was certainly a sorry chapter in my own life!

8

"Fine, Fine, Fine"

AFTER HEARING ABOUT my first husband, a fellow writer asked me, "Did you love Jim?"

"Yes, I did," I answered. "I never felt romantic love or passion with him, but I loved him like a big brother."

Like a Big Brother, Jim Gamble protected me in our early years together. As a mature man, twenty-seven years old to my twenty-two when we married, he promised to take care of me. I believed I needed that and thought it was the most I could expect from marriage. He later told my mother that I was "the *kind* of girl he wanted as a wife." I think that meant someone from a family that valued education. He applauded my intention to finish college.

Jim had already earned his university degree and was self-employed. I admired his steady, reliable character and work ethic. We had core values in common. He drank socially, as we all did, but never to excess. He kept himself clean and neat and was tidy around the house. He maintained a strong wiry body into his eighties and had a go-go energy that lasted until brain cancer took his life.

Our children and I can remember Jim's characteristic expression: "Fine, fine, fine." He always said it three times. A few years ago I read an article suggesting that someone who maintains that things are FINE is probably "Fucked up, Insecure, Neurotic and Emotionally unstable." I would not go that far in describing Jim, but he did suffer from insecurities that can be traced to his childhood.

On the other hand, his extended family contributed greatly to his strengths. Thanks to the knowledge passed along by his uncle Kenney Turk, Jim could build anything that I could design. When I won a nationwide kitchen planning contest, he transformed the room in our old farmhouse into the space I had envisioned. And he crafted clever soffit cabinets above the new metal ones that were all the rage at the time. When we dreamed of changes to other areas, he took out walls and installed new windows. If I wanted bookcases, all I had to do is sketch them and he would make them happen.

His patience extended to teaching me to drive—during our first married summer when we lived on "the Booker place." Today, when I meet women who say they can't use a stick shift, I feel grateful for those lessons in our pickup truck. My life was widened and deepened by being a farmer's wife. I learned so much that I would never have known if I'd followed my familial track into academia and wed, say, someone who went on to be a college professor. Moreover, I am grateful that I married an Oceana County man instead of a campus classmate from some other state.

My summer home of Pentwater, Michigan, was just as important to Jim as it had always been to me. His grandmother Diner's large, colonial home, with its columned front porch and backyard grape arbor played an important role in our lives while she lived. And my mother's colorful old house in the village became Jim's as much as mine. He gave many hours to its upkeep, and it was a vacation retreat for our four children as well. The North Beach cottages owned by Jim's aunts and uncles were equally familiar to me. We honeymooned in one, and, through the years, we spent many a blissful hour on the sand dunes and beach that stretched along Lake Michigan. It delights me to know that my adult children and grandchildren love spending time there today.

During the Fifties, Jim and I were active members of the Pentwater Yacht Club. That might sound ritzy, but anyone who sailed a little "Sunfish" could be a member. It was the focus of our summer social life. When Jim was elected Commodore, I was the *de facto* "Mommodore," in charge of countless dinners and dances in the clubhouse on the shore of Pentwater Lake.

We are all conditioned by the times in which we live. When we met in 1950, Jim and I were products of the postwar era, when men were again heads of households and few wives had any ambitions beyond homemaking. As long we performed in those roles, life was smooth.

Because I eventually developed great sympathy for how a childhood experience warped Jim's attitude toward physical intimacy, I hold no bitterness about what was lacking in our marriage. But it saddened me that Jim couldn't express his feelings in words. He would quote self-help authors who wrote "our feelings are as real as our nose-es and our toe-es." But he couldn't say how he felt.

213

I have no regrets about marrying Jim. I do regret the ways in which Jim and I hurt each other and our children during our twenty-seven years. I began to think about divorce long before I filed for it. A job at the *Record-Eagle* taught me that I could support myself. But, after our youngest child drowned, just before his ninth birthday, I could not bring myself to add more pain by putting our three older children through the break-up of their family.

Four years later, a "fast-talking-silver-tongued-fox" gave me the emotional strength to leave. Running away with a younger man whom I came to view as a Duke of Deception, was an unhealthy act. It hurt everyone—including me. It must be blamed on my own insecurities, not my husband's. But I've sometimes wondered what I would have done if Jim had ever said he needed me. I needed to be needed.

What he did say was, "Fine, fine, fine," as we walked out of the courthouse.

9

The Duke of Deception

FOR A FEW MONTHS after I resigned from the staff of the Traverse City Record-Eagle, I relished the rest and welcomed full time domesticity.

Just when I wondered what to do with the rest of my life, I was offered a chance to handle public relations for Northwestern Michigan College.

In addition to writing newspaper features, they asked me to design an advertising campaign. The challenge was daunting at first, but I enjoyed learning new skills. I created a series of newspaper display ads based on depicting the persons who can benefit from attending a two-year program. Each week, an attractive drawing depicted a different type of student. In addition to a recent high school graduate, readers saw faces of a returning Vietnam veteran, a housewife seeking long delayed college credit, a visual artist enrolled in studio art classes and an auto mechanic wanting to update his skills— with highlights of courses that might interest each of them.

"Great work, Judy," said Martha, my boss. "We all feel sure that our increased enrollment is directly attributable to your clever campaign."

...

Despite the success in my professional life, my home life deteriorated. Jim and I functioned politely in our domestic roles and at our elected tasks for the Unitarian Universalist Fellowship, but we were no longer intimate. When a new couple began attending Sunday services, I was attracted to their mellow lifestyle. Soon, I began to hang out with them and their friends, mostly playing cards, listening to music and drinking Gallo Burgundy. Some people smoked pot, but I never liked the taste and it gave me no high. A few guys in the crowd held jobs that paid for a roof over several others. Although not a commune, in that we didn't live together, we played musical beds. By being included, I felt wanted.

Almost daily we cooked the evening meal together, often rotating from house to house. My husband put up with it, and our 16-year-old daughter dropped in and out. She had changed her name from Cyndy (which she never liked) to Gretchen, which I loved, too. It is easy for a living parent to request a corrected birth certificate. I left Cynthia as her middle name because all her school records are in that name. I failed to realize how uncomfortable she was.

When the charismatic leader of the pack moved to California, the group dissolved and the void in my life was almost unbearable. Maybe it wasn't surprising that I fell for the silver-tongued soft-talk of a lazy hanger-on. Walt was big. Not only tall, but portly. Portly? Truthfully... fat. Just one of my women friends understood the attraction. Most people couldn't see past his belly. But his handsome face was enhanced by a small black beard and punctuated by caring dark eyes. Most importantly, he was the only man who ever made *me* feel petite. And I deserved to ride off into the sunset. That's what he said. I deserved more. *There must be more...*

So I moved with him from Michigan to Ohio. Fortunately, I did not follow through on my original plan to marry this immature alcoholic when my divorce became final. Unfortunately, I squandered most of my divorce settlement on a succession of his seemingly promising business schemes. Walt's rosy scenarios always eroded into rusty excuses.

My daughter had seemed so mature that I told myself she would be just fine without me. For a month or two, she was. But soon, her father reacted to my absence by sleeping over at the homes of eager divorcées.

"Oh Mom," Gretchen said in one of her tearful phone calls. "Dad is never home when I am. I just hate being alone every night." And a month or so later, "Mom, won't you *please* come home?"

I was more than ready.

During our 5 months in Ohio, Walt's possessiveness had trapped me in the apartment or as passenger in his car. My attempts to attend a Unitarian church service or take a college class evoked angry outbursts.

"Why do you need other people in your life?" Walt would thunder. "Why did you come with me if I'm not enough for you?"

"I don't mean to hurt you," I tried to explain. "I wish you would go with me...."

All he ever wanted to do was watch crime shows on TV—with me propped up beside him on the big bed. My pleas for understanding went unheeded. If I pressed for friends and outside stimulation, he would launch into tirades about my faults—my many faults. Seeing my tears puddle around me while he catalogued my grievous shortcomings, he would finally forgive me. As for hoping to meet new people, I gave up trying.

Meanwhile, Walt had not lasted at any job. So, when I begged him again to respond to Gretchen's heartfelt appeals, he finally agreed to return to northern Michigan.

Throughout the eighteen years I had lived in Traverse City, I had been an active supporter of the arts. Luckily, I returned to town just as the Traverse City Arts Council was seeking its first executive director. Friends on the board suggested that I apply, and my BA degree in Art History plus experience on both sides of an editorial desk landed me the job.

A realtor friend found us a sweet little house that I could afford, and Gretchen moved in with Walt and me. When he was sober, he befriended her, but he was such an overgrown child himself that he was jealous of any attention I paid to her.

"You are spoiling her rotten," was one of his milder accusations. Often he said something along the lines of "What's the use of our being together if you let her contaminate all our time? Just when we want to watch a show, you let her interrupt with some ridiculous request or other."

His jealousy never let up. He was glad I found a job and paid the bills, but if my duties required an evening board meeting, he would phone the office halfway through the designated time span, demanding to know, "How soon will you be coming home?" The one time that I accepted an invitation to go for a late drink with board members brought on such a towering rage that I never even considered it again.

He never hit me, but sometimes, if he had been drinking, he threatened to give me what I deserved. Often, late at night, he would yell, "You didn't give me enough to eat at supper. Go fix me a grilled cheese sandwich—make that two—and another Scotch on the rocks."

It may be hard to believe, but I was afraid to suggest that he do that himself. Outwardly, to friends and to colleagues at work, I appeared so capable. As I think now of how long I accepted Walt's abuse, I can only wonder at the insecurity of the woman I was back then.

One evening after supper, Gretchen placed a suitcase by the back door. As she prepared to leave for a dance class, my daughter said, "I won't be coming home, Mom. I am going to live with Gloria's family."

In the anguished conversation that followed, she explained why she was going to her girlfriend's. "I just can't stand listening to him yelling at you all the time," she said. "It hurts me to see how you put up with his drunken rages. I have to get out of here, and the Lairds have agreed to take me in."

Like a proverbial bolt of lightning, her words stabbed my heart and unleashed the truth I had to face.

"You aren't the one who'll be leaving," I told her. "Walt will. You go ahead to your dance class, and when you come home, he will be gone."

And he was.

Walt didn't argue. I owned the house. He may even have

sensed this was coming. Of course he delivered a parting crack. "Someday, when you're old 'n' gray, alone in your rocking chair, you'll look back 'n' be sorry that you ruined what we had."

Yes, he could be cruel. Yes, he used me. But I used him, too. Long unable to justify leaving my marriage, I chose to believe that I deserved to be carried off on his white charger.

Gretchen's desperation helped me to face reality. She and I lived on together in compatible camaraderie during her senior year in high school. She forgave me for what I had asked her to endure. She knew that I paid a high price for the lessons learned in that disastrous relationship.

Eventually, I summoned enough humor to look at that a year with the Duke of Deception as an expensive, post-graduate education.

Benjamin March holding baby daughter Judith at 5 months old

1929
DETROIT

Judy trying to get her mother's attention

1930
DETROIT

Judy, age 10

Engagement photo, age 21

From left: Chris (9 ½), Gretchen (4 ½), Jenny (11), Scott (1 year)
with Judy and Jim

AUGUST 14, 1965
TRAVERSE CITY, MICHIGAN

Judy, age 39

TRAVERSE CITY, MICHIGAN

Bruce, Jenny, Judy, Ethan, Gretchen, Malcolm

WEDDING DAY
MARCH 21, 1981

With Stephanie and Jason Gamble: first grandchildren

1985

"Casablanca" Party

NEW JERSEY
1990

"From the top down: Ian, Mira, Jenny, Jeremy,
Gretchen, Judy, Ethan, Leah

GRANITE DELLS IN PRESCOTT, AZ

1997

PRESCOTT, AZ
FEBRUARY 2012

Retirement from 11 years as Care Coordinator at
Granite Peak Unitarian Universalist Congregation

MAY 2014

1) Bruce Davis, 2) Dorothy Gamble, 3) Jason Gamble,
4) Chris Gamble, 5) Gretchen Hopkins, 6) Jenny Smith, 7) Jordan Davis

JUDY'S 90TH BIRTHDAY

馬

BOOK SIX

Jersey Years

*"Although almost everything in our makeup
inclines us towards the familiar, the safe
if one yearns to realize one's full potential
this can only take place in an unknown space.
For the enormity of one's potential becomes manifest
only at the awful moment when,
free from the distortion of the familiar,
away from the illusion of the safe,
you meet yourself face to face."*

– Daniel Pranger

1

Do You Remember Me?

IN SPRING, 1979, in Traverse City, I was relishing my solo life in the six months of relief after breaking up with Walt—the Duke of Deception. At age 50, I'd never lived completely alone before.

When my friend Arlo Moss called, his invitation held little appeal to me. He persisted, "C'mon Judy. Go ahead and register for Lake Geneva. Dolly and I are going. You can ride with us."

In a way it was tempting to consider another Fourth of July at the Midwest Summer Assembly. Unitarian Universalists gathered annually on the shores of that inland Wisconsin for a week of uplifting worship, enlightening workshops and fun in sun and shade. It could be a treat to reconnect with people I'd met there in earlier years. But my need for the unscheduled shenanigans had waned.

"Not this year," I told Arlo. "I've had it with the nude massage and the group grope and even the spill-your-guts all-nighters. I want to go where people are thinking about something besides themselves." My plan was to go to the U.U. General Assembly.

"The GA will be in East Lansing this June," I reminded him. "If I serve on the local arrangements committee, I can get in for a reduced fee. And I want to consider world peace and social justice and other issues beyond gazing at my own navel—or anyone else's."

So, late June found me in the early registration line for the five-day annual conference where Unitarian Universalists from across the continent gathered to do the business of the association and pass resolutions designed to influence national affairs.

Ironically, the first person I recognized was someone I'd met at Lake Geneva four years earlier. Recognizable, yes, but I couldn't come up with his name. Evan? Ian?

Do you remember me?" I asked.

"Oh yes—I do. We danced at Lake Geneva, didn't we?"

"Yes," I answered. "Danced and walked and talked. But I must confess that I don't remember your name. I'm Judy Gamble, from Traverse City, Michigan. Does that ring a bell?"

"Indeed. I remember. I'm Ethan Davis. I lived near Chicago when we met, but I'm in New Jersey now." Apparently near my age, he was good looking, about six feet tall, with wavy brown hair and crinkly blue eyes.

In 1975, I had been married to Jim Gamble. Ethan had been at Lake Geneva with his wife Abby. The four of us sat together one evening, on the edge of a dance floor. After trading partners for one number, Ethan and I silently acknowledged a mutual attraction by walking off along the lake front for a few minutes. During the next four years, we two couples exchanged cards one Christmas. Nothing more.

Standing in the registration line in 1979, Ethan explained that he had come a few days before the start of GA because, as president of the Metropolitan New York District, he was expected to attend some pre-conference meetings. Abby planned to join him when she recovered from a head cold.

During the next three days and nights, around the edges of our separate responsibilities, Ethan and I thanked our lucky stars that we had this gift of time—to update each other on our separate lives and explore that earlier attraction. He learned that I was divorced. I learned that he and Abby were seeing a marriage counselor.

Sitting side-by-side during the large plenary sessions, we chuckled over our mutual interest in such arcane subjects as bylaw amendments and general resolutions. And we spent hours alone in my dorm room.

When we returned to our respective homes, we kept in touch through letters. In July, he wrote to say that business, for his employer - the Prudential Insurance Company, would bring him to the Midwest again, and he would like to visit me. Although thrilled at the prospect of being with him again, I had deep reservations.

I knew that I was in love. But I did not want to be Ethan's exit person. I did not want to break up his home. And, an even worse scenario for me would be to hear words such as, "If it weren't for you, Judy, I would not have appreciated what I have with Abby..."

So, in response to Ethan's letter, I wrote, "If you are still trying to save your marriage, I think that you should work on that rather than coming to see *me*."

A few days later, on a Sunday afternoon, I was mowing the lawn in front of my little house on Cochlin Street. My daughter Gretchen, who was living with me during her senior year in high school, got my attention over the noise of the motor. "Ethan Davis is on the phone!" she yelled.

"Wild horses can't keep me away," he began. After I laughed with relief, he explained. "I've realized that the counseling is going nowhere with Abby. Being with you made me see how much I've been missing. I just can't continue in a loveless marriage. And I want so much to see you again."

And so, he came. I showed him the office where I worked as Executive Director of the Traverse City Arts Council, a regional arts agency. As we viewed the exhibit of Jacob Lawrence prints in the adjacent art gallery, I was amazed to hear Ethan reading aloud in French. I soon learned that he was fluent in the language because he had spent his childhood in Switzerland and France. Aha, I thought. There is more to this charming man.

Gretchen enjoyed time with Ethan and approved of our love. So did a few close friends. As it happened, I had to spend that Saturday morning at an important meeting of my Grand Traverse UU Fellowship. Remembering the "Duke of Deception's" possessiveness whenever I needed to do something without him, I feared Ethan's reaction.

"Of course, you should go to that," Ethan said. "Just drop me off at the park near the marina. I have a book I really want to read."

That evening, we were invited for dinner with Betty and Gordy Priest, who had known Walt all too well. When I told them how I'd marveled over Ethan's behavior in the morning, Gordy said, "Well, Judy, Ethan is a grown up."

The next day, we spent hours alone on a beach near the small resort village of Leland. There, while basking in the sun in our bathing suits, we affirmed our shared desire to spend the rest of our lives together

Until I met Ethan, I believed that if a man were responsible and reliable, he was also boring. And if a man were sexy and exciting, he was an irresponsible alcoholic. In Ethan, I found someone who had all the positive qualities without any negatives. He accepted me in a way that permitted me to acknowledge my feelings and act upon what I feel.

My best friend Claire commented on the level of serenity she could sense in me. "Judy, Ethan is the first man in your life who is your *equal*. You finally care enough about *yourself* to quit rescuing losers and thinking that's all you deserve."

When Ethan returned to New Jersey, he asked Abby for a divorce.

2

Honeymoon in Short Hills

THE VERY WEEK in April 1980 that Ethan and his first wife agreed to a legal separation, he noticed a posting on the bulletin board at the Unitarian Church of Summit, New Jersey.

One-bedroom apartment for rent, it said. *Attached to our home, with common front entrance.*

The apartment had been added to the attractive suburban home of Earl and Marguerite Cryer when her mother came to live with them in the pretty town of Short Hills. It offered a comfortable, convenient nest during the last few years of the mother's life. Now that it was empty, the Cryers decided to turn it into a source of income. The large living room featured a fireplace and built-in bookcases. The adjoining bedroom was almost as spacious. A bathroom and compact kitchen completed the layout.

Immediately after church service that Sunday, Ethan sought Earl. "Betty and I have decided to end our marriage, and I need to move out and find a place to live," he began.

"Would you be willing to rent me your attached apartment?"

"Certainly!" said Earl. "You'd be an ideal tenant."

Ethan happily returned to his long-ago bachelor days—shopping and cooking for himself and doing laundry. Meanwhile, he and I continued to exchange long letters as we planned for our future life together.

Life together began much sooner than we expected.

Ethan wanted me to meet his two sons who were living together in Southern Illinois. In July we arranged to visit them there. While given a brief tour of the rural property they shared, I noticed a sleek, white sports car parked alongside the house. I'd learned that both Bruce and Malcolm were expert mechanics. When I asked about the car, Malcolm explained that his hobby was restoring and refurbishing vintage Corvettes.

"I've never ridden in a sports car," I enthused, "would you be willing to take me out for a brief spin?" I saw this as an opportunity to get better acquainted with this young man.

Malcolm shook his head "no" as he looked to his father for support.

Instead, Ethan said, "oh, c'mon. It doesn't have to be a long drive..."

"Please, Dad. I just don't want to."

"Oh, just take her down to the end of your private road and back."

After a few more appeals and refusals, Malcolm finally agreed to take me out. When he saw that I was clearly enjoying the experience—more than either of us expected—he increased his speed and drove off down the country road.

I was truly thrilled, and my squeals must have encouraged him to go faster still.

As we sped up a slight hill, a red pickup truck approached from the opposite direction—in the middle of the road. Malcolm swerved right to avoid a collision and drove into a ditch—and immediately out to cross the road and end in the ditch on the opposite side.

Wearing no seatbelts, both Malcolm and I lurched sideways and piled up against the driver's door. He was unhurt, but my neck was causing severe pain. Short story: I was taken by ambulance to one hospital, transferred by helicopter to a larger hospital and outfitted with an elaborate neck brace with the misnomer of "a halo."

When Ethan asked Malcolm to visit me and apologize for the accident, he refused. I understood and reminded Ethan, "Malcolm actually saved our lives by his quick action."

"Oh, I hadn't thought of it that way—you're right. But I still wish he'd come to see you."

There was more to Malcolm's refusal than we realized. When he finally came to the hospital, he slumped sullenly in a chair and told us, "The car doesn't belong to me. I had just finished restoring it and the owner was due to pick it up the next morning. SHE (nodding toward me) cost me a bundle."

As we both gasped, Ethan had the grace to say, "Ah son, forgive me for leaning on you. But if you had only told us the situation, we wouldn't have kept urging you to give her a ride..."

Then Malcolm said more. " I don't have a driver's license," he confessed.

So, dealing with the law added to the impact of seeing the beautiful Corvette wrecked. I think he felt better after we talked it all over, and he admitted I was not to blame. So, I felt better, too. And six weeks later I was home and out of the halo.

Meanwhile, I gave up my Traverse City Arts Council job and the Cryers agreed to let me join Ethan. When he went back to work, that sweet couple helped me to learn the location of the post office, library, dry cleaners and the like. Six months later they offered to host our wedding.

Marguerite, a Home Economics teacher, helped me sew my dress—of turquoise silk faille with a cape-like collar. The wide fireplace in their living room formed a focal point for the ceremony.

Ethan's brother Curtis and his wife Julie stood up with us as our witnesses. I was delighted to meet younger brother Malcolm who agreed to come and stayed late. Ethan's two sons Malcolm and Bruce also attended, as did my two daughters Jenny and Gretchen and Curt's daughter Melissa.

My beloved aunt Lurry took the train out from Manhattan. She loved every minute of the happy occasion, plus meeting Ethan's family and my Oberlin buddy Roy Bair. He especially enjoyed meeting my girls after hearing about them in the letters I wrote over so many years.

The Reverend Scott Alexander, minister of the Unitarian Universalist Society of Plainfield conducted the ceremony featuring vows we had written ourselves. We later joined that church and remained lifelong friends with Scott.

Music was provided by a young church member who offered to play her flute. She wasn't very good, and Jenny later questioned my judgement, but I was so happy I didn't care.

The reception that followed featured a buffet dinner of beef bourginon and shrimp de jonge that I had prepared the day before. Marguerite helped to heat and serve the meal on my wedding day. Jenny baked and decorated the delicious frosted carrot cake. In retrospect, I realize we could have hired a caterer. But such a concept was completely beyond my experience, and Ethan welcomed a way to save money—without even thinking of the stress on the bride. Everyone enjoyed the meal and the chance to sit around in our apartment getting to know each other.

Ethan and I loved that apartment for ten months, until Earl explained that zoning did not really permit him to have renters. As mayor of Short Hills, he felt he could get in trouble before the coming election. We moved to half of a duplex in Westfield. The three-bedroom apartment gave us space for a home office and guests and was closer to my new job as a staff writer at the Rutgers University News Service.

Looking back in gratitude to the Cryers, we felt that our time in Short Hills couldn't have been a sweeter honeymoon.

3

How to Curtsy to a Queen

EXCITED CHATTER BOUNCED around the Rutgers University Media Relations Department that February day in 1982.

"Did you say she's coming to campus?" asked Morris, incredulously.

"Who?" asked Lorraine, who rarely paid attention to announcements.

"Yes," said Barbara Dawson, News Service Director, "As I said, Queen Beatrix of the Netherlands and her husband Prince Claus will be spending a day here in June..."

"Why?" I asked. In my ten months as a senior staff writer, I had never heard of a royal visit and certainly didn't dream of such an event.

"Their visit will be part of an east coast tour to observe two-hundred years of peaceful relations between the Netherlands and the United States," Barbara told us.

"But, why come to New Brunswick?" I persisted, between sips of my morning coffee.

"I can tell you that," answered Harvey, a longtime staffer who was well-informed about institutional history. "The Rutgers connection goes back even further—leaders of the Dutch Church in America founded the university—then called Queen's College—in 1766.

"Dutch settlers made their homes in New Jersey some three-hundred-and-fifty years ago," he explained. "And present-day residents will probably see this as a perfect opportunity to celebrate and spotlight their heritage."

The prospect of having a queen on campus was certainly a departure from the routine academic concerns I had learned to cover. Usually, our challenge was to contrive some persuasive prose that would entice the media into giving a few inches of newspaper space or three minutes of airtime to the latest research discovery or a book published by a Rutgers professor. This time, our office would be responsible for controlling and placating the reporters and photographers who would need no coaxing to descend upon us. Our boss was more than flustered. Barbara was a nail-biting wreck trying to give a good imitation of professional cool. She knew from experience how much advance work would be needed and how stressful it could become when the press demanded access to the queen.

I was about to find out for myself. To my astonishment, Barbara went on to say, "Judy, John Cooney asked me to assign you to represent our office on the overall steering committee."

"Far better you than me," snorted Morris, who looked forward to retirement within the year.

Although the thought of such responsibility was daunting, I looked forward to working with Mr. Cooney, the suave Executive Assistant for Community Relations. He wore his prematurely white hair in a luxurious pompadour above his tanned face. I had learned that he liked people who would return his teasing, and we had developed solid mutual respect.

I would be joining a team of experienced special events managers who already had several good ideas for the big day. Included in the planning were the chief of campus police, the supervisor of traffic and parking, a top-level dining hall director, representatives of the New Brunswick Theological Seminary—which was planning its own significant event—and leaders of the Holland-America Association in New Jersey.

"Your job will be to take notes during meetings. Keep track of all the ideas as they are advanced and accepted or rejected and changed," John Cooney explained. "And, once a final schedule of events is adopted, you'll need to create press advisory documents."

He didn't have to tell me that reporters and photographers would be waiting for the facts they needed in order to plan coverage by their newspapers, radio stations and television channels.

In fact, every communication needed to remind editors and news directors that, for security reasons, any representative wishing to be present during any part of the day's events had to be registered with our office in advance. They would each wear a press badge we would issue with a media kit in the designated parking lot the morning of the big day.

The weeks leading up to the queen's visit were marked by daily phone conversations between anxious Rutgers officials and suspicious Dutch security personnel. Each moment of the day had to be painstakingly mapped. Everyone had to know not only where each event would occur and when, but how the queen would be transported between locations and the names and titles of all state officials, university faculty or staff members who would be in her presence at any time.

Meanwhile, I was learning a lot about other titles. Queen Beatrix was properly addressed as "Your Majesty." Her husband was his "Royal Highness." The Ambassador Extraordinary and Plenipotentiary of the Netherlands to the United States was to be called his "Excellency," as was the State Secretary for Foreign Affairs. The Consul General of the Netherlands in New York City was called a "Jonkheer." Fortunately, he was a charming man who soon asked me to call him Leopold. His deputy described and explained most of the royal requests.

"The queen's day will start with a stop at the Theological Seminary," he said. "After a private reception, Her Majesty will open the rare books exhibit." The special collection assembled for the occasion would include historical materials about the Dutch Church in America and the founding of the university.

Then, in a lavish ceremony planned for the flower-filled college chapel, university President Edward Bloustein would present Queen Beatrix with a copy of the honorary Doctor of Laws degree which had been conferred, in absentia, on the monarch's grandmother, Queen Wilhelmina, in 1941. Due to the German occupation of her homeland at that time, the dowager queen was then living in exile in England and heard the speeches in her honor only via short wave radio.

Media arrangements for our present-day ceremony included construction of a raised platform for television crews and a mult box for both radio and TV transmission. In those uncomplicated days before computers, our office, across the street from the chapel, made all its typewriters, telephones and a telecopier available for media use throughout the day.

The luncheon to follow at President Bloustein's residence was an even greater logistical challenge. Not only were the seating arrangements of vital importance in recognizing the hierarchy of sensitive guests, but the reporters and photographers had to be fed a comparable meal in an adjacent but comfortable setting. A special bus would transport the journalists to the lunch site, and we promoted the occasion as a chance for them to meet colleagues from the Dutch media who were traveling with the queen.

The afternoon was given over to a public Holland-America Day Festival, which would transform the tree-shaded central mall on campus into a colorful outdoor marketplace lined with booths displaying Dutch arts and crafts, serving Dutch foods and displaying flowers. An estimated two thousand people enjoyed music, clog dancing and other lively, costumed entertainment.

Reporters and photographers would be expected to keep at least fifteen feet away from the queen and her consort as they made their way through the throngs of area residents with Rutgers or Dutch ties—escorted by officials and the ubiquitous secret service agents who worried as she shook hands, accepted flowers and kissed babies. A university precision drill team, known, fortuitously, as The Queens Guard, was scheduled to perform for the royal party.

By about 4 p.m., Queen Beatrix, Prince Klaus and their entourage would be driven to the nearest airport for a brief flight to Albany.

As the big day neared, most of my working hours were spent responding to reporters' calls. "No, we are really sorry, but the queen will not be granting any personal interviews… No, the queen will not be answering media questions during her day on campus…I wish I could tell you why, but we are following orders from Her Majesty's security detail….No, from what I've learned, I wouldn't count on any exceptions."

Once the queen and her party arrived, my job would be to stick with Steve Goodman, the photographer hired by our office to make an official record of the day's events for university publications and archives. Steve and I had worked together often, so we were already friends, and both knew the drill. I would point out the VIP's and he would scramble for good camera angles without trespassing on the royal space.

The team spent five weeks preparing for the queen's five hours on campus. But the morning of Monday, June 28, the one thing beyond our control was the weather.

Cloudy, windy conditions dictated a prudent change in the landing site for the queen's plane. John Cooney let me know that instead of Mercer County Airport (near Princeton), "We've decided to move it to Essex County Airport (nearer Newark). "Seems smart," he said. "Shouldn't be a problem. Everyone's been informed."

All the dignitaries had made an about face, scurried to the new location, and were lined up to greet Her Majesty's plane. First came New Jersey Governor Tom Kean, followed by Rutgers President Edward Bloustein, the New Jersey

Secretary of State Jane Burgio, Cary Edwards, chief counsel to the governor, and his family, plus university officials such as Mr. Cooney, who had masterminded the day's events.

Wait a minute! Where was Cary Edwards? His two daughters, Marcy (five) and Kari Lynn (ten) were scheduled to presen small bouquet of roses and daffodils to Queen Beatrix as she descended the steps to the tarmac. Anxiously, we shifted our gaze from the skies to the parking lot, hoping to see the Edwards family drive through the gates. But they were in Princeton.

Even as the queen's plane landed and taxied up to the assembled group, we kept hoping the children would make it in time. Unfortunately for those missing girls, who undoubtedly had been coached in curtsying, the plane door slid aside, and the lovely young queen appeared in the opening. Clad in a pretty flower-sprigged white dress and a flat-brimmed straw hat trimmed with coordinated ribbons of pink and green, Queen Beatrix smiled her way along the line of outstretched hands. From his place at the end, John Cooney cast one last look toward the parking lot, and seeing no limousine skidding to a stop, he turned and thrust the queen's bouquet into my hands!

"Here," he hissed. "Give her the flowers!"

There wasn't time to be nervous. Suddenly, there was the queen before me, with a sweet smile lighting her round, apple-cheeked face. I expected her to be the customary fifteen feet away, but she was standing right in front of me! Somehow, a long-buried snippet of information surfaced in my mind. As I offered her the bouquet, I shifted one foot back, bent my knees and curtsied to the queen!

Murmuring her thanks, she turned away toward the dignitaries, and the moment was over—a moment to be completely forgotten by everyone else, though never by me. By a happy twist of fate, my friend Steve Goodman was clicking away with his camera. He knew that a picture of me, the only inconsequential person at that airport, would not be anyone else's idea of an appropriate frame in the official record of the day. My insignificance had been the reason I was told to present the flowers. In the absence of little girls, none of the very important men there could be given the duty, and, after all, the flowers were meant for the queen. Steve knew that a picture would mean a lot to me, so he made a quick decision and caught the moment.

That photograph shares equal billing in my collected memorabilia with a copy of the letter in which Jonkheer Leopold Quarles van Ufford, the Consul General, thanked my boss for her office's "invaluable support in making the queen's visit such a noteworthy and beautiful event."

He went on to write, "The knowledgeable and efficient way that your staff took care of the publicity before and during the visit most definitely contributed largely to its success. My staff and I have personally enjoyed the pleasant cooperation."

4

Learning to Hob Nob

"JULIE JUST CALLED," I told Ethan. "She and Curt have invited us to their annual Christmas party!"

"Oh, that will be fun," he enthused. "They have so many interesting friends."

As Vice President for Programming at the Arts and Entertainment Network, Ethan's brother Curtis was well-acquainted with a variety of talented artists, musicians, producers and directors. His collaboration with Yehudi Menuhin on the book *The Music of Man* increased that celebrated circle. As Ethan's bride and a newcomer to the east coast, I had already enjoyed a few meals with Curt and Julie, who had warmly welcomed me into the Davis family.

I loved visiting their large apartment on Manhattan's West End Avenue. The pre-war building made a lasting impression on my mid-western consciousness. From the marble lobby, a private elevator rose to a small entry area outside the apartment door. Inside, a large foyer led to a long, spacious living room with a grand piano and tall windows overlooking the street. On the other side of the foyer a dining room held a table for ten plus a long buffet on one wall and, opposite, a sideboard.

The three bedrooms and baths, off an interior hallway, were shared with their teenaged children, James and Melissa. The high-ceilinged home dated to an earlier age of apartment living. A "maid's room" off the kitchen was no longer occupied by hired help.

That evening the public rooms were decorated for Christmas. Garlands of pine boughs over the broad archway and above paintings on the walls were adorned with pink and gold velvet ribbons. Arrangements of lighted candles surrounded by holly wreaths and sprigs of pine cast a comforting glow. It was a thrill for me to be part of the festive evening.

As I circulated among the guests, balancing a glass of champagne and a plate of hors d'oeuvres, I caught snippets of conversation that left me in awe of the glamourous women and distinguished gentlemen who clustered in comfortable groups. Ethan, who had earlier met a few of the celebrities, fell easily into small talk.

As the evening progressed, Julie noticed that I was at a bit of a loss. She introduced me to someone whose name and rank I no longer remember.

"It's a pleasure to meet you," said the grey-haired stranger. "Where do you live?"

When I answered, "New Jersey," I could almost physically feel, see and hear a dense curtain lower between us. "Ah… well, do have a lovely evening," said my erstwhile companion, as he moved off to join some familiar faces.

Reviewing the party with Ethan on our drive home, I described this brief encounter. Chuckling, he explained, "When a New Yorker asks that question, he wants to know if you live on the Upper West Side, where we were tonight, the Upper East Side, which has its own caché, or possibly Greenwich Village, known to the arts scene simply as "The Village.""

We laughed, content with our duplex in the tree-shaded Colonial town of Westfield, and our life that included careers in Newark and New Brunswick. But we acknowledged that New Jersey seemed beyond the pale to most of the invited guests that evening.

The following December, during the week before the annual Christmas Party, I asked Julie to tell me everything she knew about some of the guests that she was sure would attend. I took notes and memorized most of that information.

The party was as festive as before, with over-the-top refreshments and liquid libations. When one of the guests was gracious enough to strike up a conversation, I was ready.

"How do you do," he said. "Where do you live?"

"Oh, it is such a treat to meet you," I gushed. "I understand that your new opera is being produced in New Orleans next month. Would you be willing to tell me about it?"

Brightening with obvious gratification, the composer gladly described the plot and staging, continuing as I encouraged him with questions about the soloists and the company that had invited him to perform his work.

Assessing me as a worthwhile companion, he eventually asked me what I "did" and even expressed some interest in my work as a senior staff writer at Rutgers. He may soon have remembered where the university was located, but by then that didn't matter.

As the years passed, Curt and Julie's parties became more and more pleasurable for me. I enjoyed what I learned from the talented guests, and I managed to finesse each encounter so that a lot of information was exchanged before someone realized that we lived in New Jersey.

5

Rutgers Newark

In 1987 I was promoted to the position of Director in the Newark office of Rutgers' Public Information Department. My ego was massaged and the job appealed to me for superficial reasons—such as an attractive corner office on the thirteenth floor of the Law School building, with a magnificent view of the Manhattan skyline across the Hudson River.

I liked the Newark Campus. In a more casual atmosphere, professors were apt to request "Call me Bob," instead of insistence on the "doctor" honorific that a Ph.D. merited.

As I gained knowledge of the city, I appreciated the multi-cultural mix of residents. Ethnic restaurants became frequent destinations. One of my staff writers, Erma Brown, who was of Portuguese heritage, steered us to her favorites.

Another advantage of the Newark job was that Ethan and I could drive to work together—in contrast to the six years he took a bus or train while I drove our car to the main campus in New Brunswick. In Newark I dropped him off at the Prudential building before going a few blocks further. We often met friends for dinner.

I felt important, but the responsibilities of directorship included developing departmental budgets and other onerous managerial tasks. The university bigwigs held tightly to purse strings.

"I can't even get my secretary a raise," I complained to Ethan. "You know how well Diane deserves it. I want to do right by her." She still had a tender chip on her shoulder over losing her old boss.

"Have I told you I hate management?" I whined.

"A few times," answered my patient husband who had been in management positions his entire career. "What did you expect?"

I missed writing. If I wanted to assign myself a magazine feature, I had to stay late into the evening or take the work home. I enjoyed the results enough to do that often and endure fatigue.

Another aspect of management was that the buck always stopped with me. Professors believed that if I could get their work covered by the *New York Times* often enough, they would win the Nobel Prize—or at the very least, they would receive the grant money they deserved. I did call the *New York Times*, of course.

"Is this cutting-edge research?" a *Times* editor would ask.

"Well, not exactly," I had to admit.

"Well, call us back when it is."

One event on the Rutgers-Newark campus did merit

a spread in the *Times*. A national Poetry Conference. Public readings drew surprisingly large audiences, with complimentary letters to the editor in the local paper—the Newark *Star-Ledger*.

The second year on the job, I needed to fill a vacant staff writer position. Reviewing applications and interviewing prospective candidates took many hours. I gave the tasks a lot of attention, but I misjudged one of the women I spoke with. Comparing her with my energetic daughter of about the same age, I thought she would be a bright capable addition to the department.

Wrong. Lauren's pert good looks and open friendliness won over many faculty members, but she ignored my instructions, was lazy with assignments and turned in sloppy work late.

"She's making us all miss deadlines," complained Erma, the veteran senior staff writer. "I must admit I had serious reservations about her in the first place. I thought she was putting on a show. And now I worry about the way she's affecting media perceptions of our office."

I agreed with her. "You're right. The *Star-Ledger* editor called to say our press release was too late for today's edition."

Dealing with the cute junior staff member dominated my life for months. Frequent confrontations went something like this:

"Lauren, I'm having to spend way too much of my own time correcting your writing. You are careless in your work."

"But you told me I was late turning in assignments," she protested. "So I couldn't take time to check things."

"I know you enjoy schmoozing with some of the

instructors," I said, "But you've got to learn to manage your time. I'll be glad to help you…"

Explanations went over her head, and her excuses annoyed me more and more. Other demands of my work began to feel like burdens. I began to wish that my standards weren't so high. I wished I could quit. I asked myself, what are my options?

You could quit.

You could let things slide.

You could refuse coverage requests from faculty members and risk their complaints to the higher ups.

You could turn down personal writing, so you'd get more sleep.

You could continue to rewrite Lauren's assignments and continue the daily frustrations.

Then I learned of an option I hadn't known existed. Early retirement. Staff members could retire at age sixty. I had turned sixty in January. I applied to leave after commencement in June.

If I had been self-supporting, I could not have afforded to make that choice, but, luckily, Ethan's salary from The Prudential kept a roof over our heads and food on the table. And he supported my decision. Moreover, one advantage of having been in management was eligibility for a TIAA pension.

The campus Provost called me into his office to tell me, "Judy, I'm really sorry you're going to leave us. I know the job is demanding. But you are an excellent writer, so I hope you'll accept stories for the *Rutgers Alumni Magazine*. How about seeking commercial magazine work as well?"

That I did, and I feel proud of my freelance writing during the next few years.

Ethan was pleased to see me happy again. But he was envious. When he had to drive off alone in the mornings, he began to imagine his own life without the daily commute and demands of his job. He took accumulated vacation time for our bucket list foreign travel, and eventually he followed my lead and decided to retire at sixty-two.

Two years later we visited Prescott, Arizona and soon moved into my dream house in that ideal town.

馬

BOOK SEVEN

Westward Ho

*"Along the way the self you were born with
turns into the self that you created,
but they come together in the end."*

– John Koethe

1

Retirement

"WHY DID YOU PICK Prescott for retirement?" we were often asked—starting in June 1996.

Four season climate. Middle-sized town with three colleges and an active arts scene. Unique natural surroundings. Ethan's son Bruce discovered it and, knowing we wanted to move to the Southwest, phoned us in New Jersey to say, "You guys gotta check this out."

We agreed with his assessment and lucked out at house-hunting. "Skyridge" was my dream house. While lacking elegance, it held natural features that gave it special charm. What I saw from the front door nearly convinced me this was our new home then and there.

A soaring stone fireplace reached a cathedral ceiling. A thick wooden banister bordered the staircase rising *behind* the fireplace! Two living room walls of windows were outfitted with wooden plantation blinds. A "Juliet" balcony opened off the upstairs master bedroom through a louvered door and led outside to a small upper deck. The lower deck held our picnic table and benches. Once a roadrunner hopped up to peck at his reflection in the living room window. Javelina frequented the space, once recruiting long lost cousins when the bottom fell out of our birdfeeder.

...

I expected to write free-lance articles for local and regional magazines, and that we would both join the Prescott U.U. Fellowship. We thought. But we came to town the very month that eighteen members of PUUF resigned with a goal of establishing a full-service church. We threw our weight with them. The work of creating a new congregation, managing its finances and conducting worship services dominated our lives for several years. The Granite Peak Unitarian Universalist Congregation continues to be central to my life.

I also volunteered as a docent at the Sharlot Hall Museum. I enjoyed guiding visitors in the old log Governor's Mansion and spent every Tuesday in the Fremont House, describing anything anyone wanted to know about the fifth territorial governor. Ethan joined me to sell commemorative tee shirts at the Indian Art Market every year for ten years.

I also became active with the group called Yavapai HIV-AIDS Action—people supportive of those infected or affected by the epidemic disease. Over the following fifteen years, I served as clinic coordinator, board secretary and president. After the organization became known as Northland Cares, I continued as an office volunteer once a week.

...

Early in our retirement, we went river rafting through the
Grand Canyon. Subsequently, I answered an appeal for
advice from a perspective voyager:

*You are in for an awesome experience!!! We took an
'Edventure' conducted by the local Yavapai Community
College, which contracted with the Hualapai Indians for the
two days of rafting and meals at stops along the river. The full
week-long program included hikes and lectures by excellent
college faculty members—on the geology of the canyon and the
fascinating history of the native peoples and all the early river
expeditions. You will be on the river much longer and cover a
much greater distance, so it should be perfectly wonderful! If
your Expeditions company does not offer any 'education' about
what you are seeing, you may want to read in advance. It will
all mean more to you, I think. You probably know about John
Wesley Powell etc.*

*As for practical suggestions—you will probably live in
a bathing suits and tee-shirt—or long-sleeve shirts if you
prefer, to prevent sunburn. A wide-brimmed hat that **ties
on** would be good—and those special cords to secure your
sunglasses around your neck. Some people wore light weight
shorts over their bathing suits. It was more modest, I guess,
but not strictly necessary. You will be drenched much of the
time, but will dry off very quickly, and soon be so hot that
you will welcome the next set of rapids to cool you off! If
you own a pair of those 'splash shoes' that are advertised for
water aerobics and rocky beaches, those would be perfect—
but an old pair of sneakers would be just a good—worn
without socks of course. The canyon "beaches" are rocky and*

you will want to walk back into side canyons to see gorgeous waterfalls etc.

The greatest surprise, for us, was that the river water was just like chocolate milk, and when it dried on our skin, we all looked ke ancient "mud men!" Fresh water for washing was limited, so when we stopped for the evening, most of us just tended to our faces and private parts and let the arms and legs be…. But we only slept out in the canyon **one night**—*and it was so hot that we lay on top of the sleeping bags—so it didn't matter. For eight days, your Expeditions company will surely provide a way to wash off at night.*

The experience of sleeping out deep in the canyon will be thrilling!! Because there is **no** *light in the Inner Gorge, every star in the firmament is visible—simply astonishing!!! Lying there, looking up before I fell asleep, I felt something skitter across my bare legs. Whether a mouse or a small snake, no telling. It hastened away.*

People often ask us about "potty" stops—so you may be curious too. Urination must be done in the river, and for women this is a real challenge!! Wearing a bathing suit helps, but the banks are muddy, the current swift! If you can allow yourself to pee in your bathing suit in the raft **while** *shooting the rapids, everything including your body will be washed in the process! You will be told that everything that is carried into the canyon must be carried out, and that includes human waste! We each carried an empty coffee can which could be dumped into the porta-potty at night and then rinsed in the river. I hope this isn't more than you wanted to know.*

...

A trans-Atlantic cruise wasn't even on my bucket list, but in May 1998, Rena Bain, a widowed friend who needed a female companion for such an excursion, offered to pay half my fare. Ethan had experienced ocean crossings as a boy, so he gave us his blessing and managed just fine at home—with a few meals gifted by friends.

The cruise lasted seventeen days, from Miami, with stops in the Canary Islands, Madeira, Morocco, Alicante and Ibiza, to Barcelona, where we had two extra days before flying home. And, for my first ever cruise, I certainly "started at the top!" The Cunard liner "Vistafjord" is a lovely classic ship, operated in an upper crust British style, with a very friendly crew of 409 (from forty countries) serving 545 passengers.

I must admit that I enjoyed all the luxuries—but ocean crossing is an interesting combination of pampered living, with one's every whim indulged, AND a certain tedium after 7 days at sea! Five days were cold and cloudy, so I had the feeling of being "trapped" in that elegant floating resort, and I looked forward to reaching ports. Rena played bridge every day, so she hardly cared where she was. To other passengers, the ports were a distraction to the delights of an idle lifestyle, and some people did not even go ashore!!

Rena's demands made me feel like a Sherpa. But I felt that I earned my passage. I only wish Ethan had been along for dancing. Most other women were fiercely opposed to lending their husbands.

The trip confirmed my preference for special occasions spread out, not lumped together for seventeen straight days! And although we had good luck to be assigned compatible dinner table companions who helped to celebrate Rena's eighty-eighth birthday, eating with the same eight people night after night was a social challenge!

...

Back in Arizona, I volunteered as a docent at Prescott's Sharlot Hall Museum. I enjoyed guiding visitors in the old log governor's mansion and spent every Tuesday in the Fremont House, describing anything anyone wanted to know about the fifth territorial governor. Ethan joined me to sell commemorative tee shirts at the annual Indian Art Market.

2

An Earthshaking Wedding

BRUCE DAVIS, my stepson, and his girlfriend Lisa agreed on one thing. After nine years together, they were ready for marriage. But their discussions about where and when and how to wed dragged on for weeks—punctuated by raised voices, shared frustrations and a few tears.

Neither of them wanted a lavish traditional wedding. Lisa thought that the two of them could just go by themselves, find a judge and be done with it. Bruce wanted a little more. Nothing fancy, but an occasion with a sense of celebration and some family and friends there. Most of all, he wanted it to be *fun.*

That's when he came up with the idea of Las Vegas! He invited his dad and me to clear our calendars for Saturday, October 16, 1999. Three longtime friends of his from Illinois were going to be in Vegas that weekend and could also attend a wedding. Still nothing was definite until noon Friday when Lisa finally agreed to do it Bruce's way. They managed to reserve reasonably priced rooms for the night, and at ten p.m. the four of us embarked on a mellow four hour drive from Arizona to Nevada.

Despite fatigue, our first sight of the fantasy city put us in the mood for fun. From a hill beyond Hoover Dam sparkling golden lights stretched out to seemingly endless horizons, beckoning us to the playground of gamblers and lovers.

The Rio Casino Resort turned out to be a glitzy high rise, gleaming in red and blue neon against the night sky. When we checked in at 2:15 a.m. the desk clerk confessed to having given away our reserved non-smoking rooms and offered us an "upgrade." To our amazement, we were given vast corner suites, each complete with a bar in the living room, walk-in closet, bath and a half, and a jacuzzi tub set into a window alcove of the bedroom.

We had barely explored the place when, at 2:45, we had another surprise: the aftershock of the Joshua Tree earthquake. The major California quake, measured at 7.0, set our whole building heaving, swaying and rattling. In awe at our first such experience, we marveled open-mouthed— and by the time we wondered if we should evacuate, the trembling was over. Meanwhile, Bruce had wasted no time in pulling Lisa outside. Leaving all possessions, including keys and billfolds, they fled down a dark stairwell.

When he phoned to see if we were all right, I teased him about making such vigorous whoopee that they shook the whole hotel. His laugh was a bit strained because, wearing nothing but cargo shorts, he was trying to persuade the desk clerk to let them back into their high roller suite.

...

By mid-morning, Ethan and I were wondering when and where the wedding would take place. But Bruce and Lisa were in no hurry. So we agreed to order breakfast for four delivered to their suite, where we enjoyed the luxury of a private meal with expansive views toward distant mountains.

Since we had to check out of paradise by one o'clock, a noon reminder finally motivated Bruce to call to reserve a hotel wedding chapel. There was an opening at 5:30, but a bride and groom were required to show their marriage license before reserving the space. A marriage license! So, we all dressed, checked out and made our way to the Municipal Marriage Bureau, which stays open twenty-four hours on weekends.

While Lisa and Bruce stood in line inside, Ethan and I waited outside in the mild weather. Sitting on a low wall, we took in the parade of couples—young, old, black, white, dressed in lace or tee shirts, jubilant or business-like, smooching or shyly self-conscious—a never-ending flow coming and going from the building, all clutching their precious permits.

Back at the hotel we saw a traditionally clad bride dashing through the crowded casino with her mother trotting frantically along behind, holding up a long satin train. Another young woman had clearly come from a beauty salon. Her thick dark hair was pulled up into a fancy topknot surrounded by a sparkling tiara from which flared a shoulder length veil. From the neck up she was a vision. From the neck down a sight—still in her denim shorts and crop top!

License in hand, Bruce and Lisa ordered a no-frills Protestant wedding ceremony. No pianist, no cascading bouquet, no professional photographs or video, no honeymoon suite. But later, while Bruce was having a drink with his buddies around the swimming pool and Lisa was playing the slot machines, I sought a florist. No frills can't mean no flowers, I reasoned. Some small gesture was needed.

Michael, the floral designer, was delighted to be in on the surprise. He couldn't have been sweeter in agreeing to deliver his creation to the chapel. Everyone later agreed that the slim arrangement of peach-colored roses, stephanotis and ivy resting on Lisa's forearm relieved the stark simplicity of her plain dark blue dress and added a touch of romance.

While waiting around the Rio Casino that afternoon, we took in the scene. On two levels, arcaded shop fronts were designed to look like a "Tuscan Village." How a hotel named Rio adopted for a faux Italian theme remains a mystery. Then, nearly deafened by the canned music and the beeping, clanging and chiming of slot machines, we watched in wonder as an upper façade, painted on canvas, was lowered to reveal a huge Mardi Gras balloon—the head of a veiled harem girl—which floated (OK, moved on a track) out over the gamblers and seething throngs below. When a three-story stage rose up from beneath the floor, a dozen energetic entertainers appeared in colorfully sequined costumes. Their dancing was delightful, but the singing was wasted. The volume of the amplification made the lyrics unintelligible. Meanwhile, the ceiling tracks now carried a gilded Viking ship and a glittering Mississippi river boat, both showcasing other entertainers. So much for unified theme.

The trousers that Bruce planned to wear for his wedding had been left at home, so he talked of finding a mall where he could buy a new pair. But, he decided to play the slot machines with Lisa instead. Ethan and I found a cocktail lounge where we ordered daiquiris and appreciated the lower noise level.

By four fifteen, the bride-to-be needed a little real food in her nervous tummy, and "lunch" sounded good to us, too. While well-seasoned Italian salads were being prepared, the groom went up the escalator to check out the men's clothing stores. Rejecting the $200 price tags, he decided that his faded jeans would have to do—enhanced by a favorite soft white shirt and cowboy boots.

Next came the appointed meeting with the minister—in a tastefully decorated lounge featuring glass-topped coffee tables and sofas upholstered in peach and green tapestry. Lighted display cabinets held beribboned champagne flutes, satin and lace covered guest books and photo albums, silver candlesticks and cake servers—all the accessories one might desire for a reception in the Lilly of the Valley room.

The coordinator for the Miller-Davis wedding was a peppy named Kelly. She managed a valiant balance between sticking to protocol and going with the flow.

"Who will be your attendants?" she asked.

Lisa had never even thought about it and didn't think she needed one until she learned that Bruce had asked his friend Mike to be his best man. Glancing my way, she murmured, "Maybe Judy could do it." I meant it when I said I'd love to.

While the bridal couple was closeted with the minister, Ethan and I looked around the Gardenia Chapel, which held fifty chairs painted peachy beige to match the woodwork. Five arched openings across the front of the room were fitted with etched glass panels. On either side of a low platform two tall faux marble urns held lavish silk arrangements of peach and white lilies, peonies, snap dragons and apple blossoms. My choice of peach roses for Lisa seemed meant-to-be. Soft classical music played over a speaker system while we waited for the show to begin.

As it turned out, both of Bruce's bosses, one wife and two co-workers made a last-minute decision to drive up from Phoenix for his wedding. Their presence was a surprise to Lisa, who, in the end, was glad of a few more guests.

But they were late. By 5:40, Kelly became a little shrill, reminding us that another wedding was scheduled in that chapel at six.

Soon our party assembled. As instructed, Mike offered me his arm. If this smiling blonde boy thought we made an incongruous pair, he gave no hint of it. He even quipped that he hoped he got to kiss the "maid-of-honor." If Lisa was sorry that she put me in this position, it was too late. Just one more compromise in this astonishing day.

Despite its relative brevity, the ceremony never felt rushed—thanks to the warmth and skill of the clergywoman whose practiced words were spoken with sincerity and joy. One might have thought she had known this man and woman all their lives. The vows were creative adaptations of conventional phrases.

Not surprisingly, Bruce hadn't remembered to buy a ring. So, in advance, Lisa removed her engagement band. As directed by the minister, Bruce replaced it on her finger. They were pronounced husband and wife, recessed to traditional music, and it was all over but the snapshots.

Since Ethan and I had to drive home that night to keep an early Sunday commitment, Bruce and Lisa arranged to stay over, crash on Mike's sofa and ride back with him. This offered them the chance to party with friends as Bruce envisioned.

When Bruce came to our car to see us off, he spoke genuinely of his gratitude and pleasure that we had been with him for this special moment in his life. His procrastination is a lifelong habit, and such details as missing pants and rings didn't matter to him, or, apparently, to Lisa.

I couldn't help wishing that Lisa's parents had been there. Bruce did invite his mother and brother, but not until Friday afternoon, practically assuring that she would feel it was too short notice to drive from San Diego. Still, she was glad to be told about it, and we were glad she knew.

So, in the end, everything came off just as Bruce hoped it would, and Lisa seemed content with the result. It certainly was a joy for us to participate in that unique occasion. None of us will ever forget their *Earthshaking* wedding.

3

The Queen Buff

THE NATURAL QUESTION WAS, "What is your connection with Frank Lloyd Wright?"

The people assembled at Taliesin West, the late architect's home and studio in the desert near Scottsdale, were there to "Celebrate the Legacy." They looked forward to participating in some or all of the four-day October 2004 fund raiser hosted by the Frank Lloyd Wright Foundation.

My husband Ethan and I were there for one special day to be capped by a Gala Moonlight Dinner. We would be among 385 guests to hear the acclaimed television producer Ken Burns describe the making of his new documentary about the man he characterized as "America's Greatest Architect." We felt privileged to view the film before it was to be telecast on PBS, and to meet Burns, who proved to be a warm, unpretentious guy.

Using his tested formula of combining period photographs with contemporary interviews, the filmmaker described how

Wright fell in love with Arizona in the 1930's when he came to escape the cold of his native Wisconsin winters.

Taliesin West, a sprawling complex with unique native stone exterior walls and soaring broad wooden beams, was hand-constructed by young apprentices who studied under the master. The low-slung structures suited the environment—a key aspect of the architect's work that gained him such fame.

Another assignment for each apprentice had been to design and build a small, individual shelter that would be his or her home for the winter. Some of those students stayed on to live and work there for years. Now, decades later, others had returned from far and wide for this special event.

As guests, we were all understandably curious about each other. We wondered what motivated the young and the old, the very rich and the not-so-rich, those in shorts and sockless sneakers, those who affected artsy all-black attire, and especially those who had used vacation days to fly in from New Hampshire, Georgia, Illinois, Louisiana—even Scotland and Japan!

Which of us was an artist or architect? Which a journalist or a screen writer or photographer? Which a major philanthropist? Which was a former student of Wright's or an owner of a home designed by the gifted genius we were all there to honor and remember?

When asked, I responded simply, "I guess you could say that I'm a Frank Lloyd Wright *buff*."

I became a fan of his work when I studied the history of architecture at Oberlin College. Independently, I went on to study his work, visit his houses and public buildings, and admire his theories. When I moved to Arizona in 1996, I became a member/supporter of the Foundation. I thought "buff" pretty well described my amateur devotion.

At the luncheon table, my answer seemed to please Connie, the friendly young architect from Denver. A pretty brunette, she was on her way, with her husband, to buy land along the Big Sur coast of California. After describing her work, she seemed genuinely sympathetic when I confided, "When I was in school, I didn't know that girls could become architects!"

Feeling a need to include other guests in our conversation, we politely turned to the woman across the table. "And what fostered your interest in Wright's work?" I asked.

Dressed in a low cut white knit tank top over pink cropped pants, flashing diamonds as she gestured, the chubby bleached blonde—sixty-something—looked and sounded like a coarse, brassy B-movie actress. In fact, she was an interior decorator from Atlanta who claimed to have *built and lived in six* Frank Lloyd Wright houses!

"I act as my own contractor," she explained to her astonished audience, as she took another sip of her gin and tonic. "I don't trust those ordinary builders to do things right. So I supervise the construction and sub-contract the work."

After living in a house for a few years, she added, "I would get itchy to build another one." Each time, she adapted the original Wright plans to her own needs and contemporary architectural ideas. After thirty years of this, she made enough selling houses to give up her decorating business.

"I got sick of working in the gaudy styles most clients wanted," she proclaimed. "Most people have no taste at all!"

Fran and her husband, whose portly build and distinguished grey hair could have belonged to a banker or a stockbroker—we never found out—have lived in their current home more than five years. "That's the longest she's been content," observed the smiling man, who seemed accustomed to indulging his wife's whims.

"But now I want to build one more house," said Fran. "It will be the best. I already have the property picked out, and I figure I can build it for about $500,000 and sell it for a million and a half. Then I want to use the money to travel— to Frank Lloyd Wright sites and events like this one—and to create a Frank Lloyd Wright visitors center in Atlanta."

As the rest of us, open-mouthed, took this all in, Fran's husband described her extensive library of books on Wright that would form the nucleus of displays at the center. "My dream," she told us, "is to create a southeastern branch of the Frank Lloyd Wright Foundation."

Wow! I thought. Someone else whistled softly.

Later, as I pushed back my chair to leave the luncheon table, I leaned over to Connie and whispered, "I guess I can't really call myself a buff after all!" Tilting my chin toward Fran, I said, "Now *there's* a buff!"

"The Queen Buff," laughed Connie.

...

Today, I remain curious about whether Fran ever carried out her plan to build a Wright visitors center/library in Atlanta. Google reveals no such structure. She was not the only fan in that city. Several links to the master architect came up. But nothing resembling the center she envisioned.

I like to imagine that an even more intriguing concept hooked her instead.

4

The Million Dollar Photograph

MY FATHER, Ben March, was a talented amateur photographer. He also collected photographs taken by others. Many mounted and matted photos were stored in large flat boxes covered with dark blue cloth—boxes that were among his belongings that I inherited and kept, unexamined.

My last job in Traverse City Michigan was as executive director of the regional Arts Council. My boss, the board chairman Ann Ozegovic, was a photographer herself, so, before I moved to New Jersey in 1980, I asked her to look through the old photos and try to evaluate their worth.

In the lot, she recognized one by Edward Weston. The name meant nothing to me, but Annie thought, "It might be valuable." She offered to find out and I left it with her, along with a few prints by my father and others. She never followed up on her offer, and I never reminded her about it. Every once in a while, Ethan would ask me; "Did you ever hear from Annie O. about the photographs she kept?" But

I didn't want to bother her about it.

Nine years later, when she and Jack were preparing to leave Traverse City themselves, they decided to donate a batch of photographs, including mine, to the fledgling Dennos Art Museum on the campus of Northwestern Michigan College, where Jack had been an art instructor. When they sought my permission, I thought it was a great idea and readily agreed. All three of our names were on the acquisition form for the donation.

In the spring of 2008, Eugene Jenneman, director of the then-established small museum, happened to watch a television show about how the "nouveau riche" spend their money. A reporter described an art auction at Sotheby's New York, at which a photograph by Edward Weston, renowned California photographer, had sold for 1.6 million dollars. It was one of only five classic photographs to sell for more than a million. Gene Jenneman nearly choked when he recognized the artful photo of a supine nude woman's torso as a duplicate of the one owned by his museum—the one I donated.

When he contacted me, our astonishment was equaled by chagrin over my ignorance and failure to nudge Ann about what she took. Signed and dated, the photo I had owned turned out to be one of four large format contact prints made by Weston in 1925. Unlike pictures developed from a negative, contact prints are created once, by the artist. No more can ever be made.

Of the four nude images, one is in the Metropolitan Museum of Art, one is somewhat damaged, the third is the one that was bid up so high at Sotheby's, and the fourth was mine. While printed at the same time, each photo was slightly different in quality and condition. But after the incredibly high price paid at auction, all became more valuable.

Eugene Jenneman hoped that I would know how my father came to possess one print of the photograph. From 1927 to 1933, Ben March was curator of Far Eastern Art at the Detroit Institute of Arts. During those years, he was also a well-respected amateur photographer who won many awards and served as a judge for major shows. After his untimely death in 1934, his work was boxed up and stored by my mother. I didn't go through those boxes until after her death in 1969, and it was another ten years before I asked Ann Ozegovic to tell me what I had.

It is possible that Ben March knew Edward Weston. They could have met when Weston exhibited in Detroit during that period. The print of the Weston "Untitled Nude" that Ben possessed was stamped on the back with the name of Merle Armitage, a well-known art dealer. Whether either Weston or Armitage gave it to Ben or Ben bought it from Armitage, we have no way, now, of knowing.

But, for the director of a small art museum in northern Michigan, having such a rare copy was a very big deal. Thrilled, Gene Jenneman immediately began planning an appropriate celebration. He had the photo reframed and hung in a prominent place, with a similarly framed description of the provenance, including my father's name and my own as one of the donors.

He also arranged a gala reception featuring an illustrated lecture by a Sotheby's expechief counsel to the governorrt on photography. When we received an invitation for the June 26th event, Ethan said, "Oh, we must go!"

I had sworn that I wouldn't go back to Michigan in the summer again because my son, Chris Gamble and his wife are so busy running their motel at that time of year that we could not expect to have much meaningful time with them. And, the last time I had been in Traverse City, the astonishing urban sprawl and growth of "sophisticated" establishments offering outrageously expensive wines and tapas left me feeling quite alienated.

But Ethan felt that the celebration over the photo would be a "once in a lifetime" affair that we shouldn't miss. So, we called Ann and Jack Ozegovic at their home in Lawrence, Kansas, and persuaded them to come and share in the fun and fame.

It was indeed a memorable evening. The crowded reception in the museum's spacious lobby sculpture court offered champagne and elegant hors d'oeuvres. In Milliken Auditorium, the lecture by Christopher Mahoney, senior vice president of Sotheby's Photographs Department, provided fascinating insights into the reasons for Edward Weston's fame. One of the "blue chip" modernists in the early 20th century, Weston was particularly renowned for his sensual treatment of such subjects as sea shells, sweet peppers and other organic forms, as well as female nudes.

The entire evening turned out to be a delight. Not only did we enjoy the reunion with Jack and Ann, another old friend of mine drove up from Midland. His wife is a prominent supporter of the arts. When he saw my name on the invitation she received, they decided to surprise us at the reception. Eugene Jenneman had willingly added two special Traverse City friends to the guest list, and it was heartwarming to see local artists and other members of the Arts Council, who remembered me from my years at the helm.

Chris and Dorothy Gamble were even able to take time off from their duties at the Ludington Pier House to help us celebrate at "The Event." They had to leave following the lecture and reception at the museum, but the president of Northwestern Michigan College treated a small group of us to late-night supper at the Traverse City Country Club. This gave us time to ask the expert from Sotheby's what he thought our Weston print might have been worth.

Chris Mahoney told us that, in 1980 another Edward Weston picture, of a seashell I believe, broke the mark of $100,000 at auction—the first photograph by any artist to bring that high a price. Therefore, Mahoney estimated, had my Weston photo been appraised that year, instead of my giving it to Ann Ozegovic, it might have been worth about $85,000.

Friends wondered if we could claim a tax deduction for our gift to the museum. But a tax accountant told us that there is a three-year limitation on such a benefit from a charitable contribution. Oh well.

During the next several days, we saw many other old friends. We were led to appreciate the changes in Traverse City through the eyes of local residents who rejoice in them. We certainly understood their excitement over the annual film festival organized and hosted by Michael Moore. The famous—or infamous—film maker had used his own money to finance a stunning restoration of a downtown theater.

As a newly celebrated "philanthropist" myself, I was assured of belonging. Most importantly, we rejoice over our role in putting a small mid-western art museum on the map.

5

Caring About AIDS

WHEN WE LIVED IN NEW JERSEY, I'd learned about a life-threatening disease called AIDS. A close friend, Roy Bair, was devoting many hours to "buddying" young men—helping them through the medical maze and arranging for financial support when they became too sick to work. During those years when contracting HIV/AIDS was a death sentence, Roy was able to cry with us over the loss of far too many of his buddies.

Meanwhile, a close friend of my daughter's moved to New York City and spent many holidays with us. KC was very busy in his nursing training, but when too long a time had gone by without hearing from him, I left messages begging him to call. Finally, in anguish, he had to tell me, "Judy, I have AIDS." When he became too sick to manage alone, KC moved back to Michigan, where his family cared for him while he lost his mind before he lost his life.

During those years, I gave money but didn't know how

to get personally involved until I met a woman who, with her husband, founded homes for babies and toddlers with HIV/AIDS. These two wonderful people, both physicians in Newark, had seen too many wee ones languishing in hospital wards, their mothers dead or dying and without relatives willing to risk caring for them!! So, they appealed to donors to help them buy houses where these children could live, and hired staff to care for them. They also needed volunteers, so, when I retired, I offered to come in two days a week.

Some of my friends were appalled. They not only feared for my own health, but they assumed that such work would be terribly sad. On the contrary, those St. Clare's Homes for Children were bright, happy places where adults did all they could to make the kids' lives as joyful as possible for as long as possible. Yes, some of the babies I rocked and the toddlers I played with died. And yes, we all grieved. But I loved being a surrogate grandma and it was so heartwarming when families bravely stepped up to adopt or foster some of the children.

Soon after Ethan and I moved to Prescott in 1996, I met Marriner Cardon, who was on the board of Yavapai HIV/AIDS Action, the organization that eventually evolved into Northland Cares. When he learned what I'd been doing in New Jersey, he said, "Do I have a job for *you!*"

YHAA was originally formed by parents whose sons had died. They recognized a need for support for those affected by the disease as well as those infected. But, in Prescott there was also a need to offer medical care. Dr. Sam Downing was the first physician to treat patients with AIDS. Thanks to him and case manager Nancy Rees, YHAA was able to provide a monthly clinic for those seeking treatment. Over the years, I served as secretary of the board, president of the board, coordinator of "lay" volunteers who assisted the professional volunteers at the clinic and covered shifts in the YHAA office before we had any paid staff.

I wish that there was no longer a need for an organization to serve people infected or affected by HIV in this area. But as long as that need continues, I give thanks for the opportunity to contribute through Northland Cares. In 2010 I was recognized as the first non-professional to receive the Dr. Samuel Downing World AIDS Day Community Impact Award for "Exemplary service, unwavering dedication and deep compassion for people living with HIV/AIDS in Northern Arizona."

6

Birthing *Pagoda Dreamer*

"Is THIS *YOUR* STORY or your mother's?" she asked.

Karen Anderson, a talented professional writer and good friend, had offered to edit the first draft of a book I hoped to publish. We were together in her home, in Traverse City, Michigan—sitting in her familiar kitchen. A white-painted table and matching benches formed the nook where we reviewed my manuscript.

"It's Doré's story," I answered, knowing that she understood my motivation and recognized my mother's nickname. The impetus for this book-to-be was a cache of letters. My mother was the author of four chapter books for children. Her talent with words also informed her letters. Back in the day, when many people wrote long letters to distant relatives, Doré regularly described her days and her dreams to her beloved sister Louise. This sister, nicknamed Lurry, saved those letters for fifty years—and left them for me after her death.

"If the book is to be told from your mother's point of view," Karen continued, "then I suggest you cut passages that describe experiences as you saw them. Such as this place... and this one...and again here in the following section."

With kindness as well as wisdom, Karen explained that describing my own reactions to experiences I had shared with my mother did not enhance the biography of her that I was trying to write. As a former English teacher, columnist and essayist, she brought both expertise and insight to her comments on my work.

The story was written in my voice as the daughter. Whenever my health or my life decisions burdened or delighted my mother, those times had to be included. But not my separate, personal experiences during the same time periods.

I got it.

In 1986, I found the big box of letters in Lurry's New York apartment. I was delighted to have them but had no idea what to do with them. I took the box home and stashed it in our New Jersey garage. On my seventieth birthday in 1999, I read the letters. And concluded that they were too beautiful to destroy or to leave to be destroyed after my death. I continued to save them.

By 2008, I had taken excerpts from the letters and put them into a narrative to tell my mother's story. In Karen's kitchen, her next suggestion was that I tell more about Lurry. "After all," she pointed out, "besides *you*, Lurry was the most important person in Doré's life." Although separated by the Pacific Ocean, their correspondence kept the sisters connected. It began when Doré was back in China after college and Lurry had just entered Goucher College in Baltimore. Her career years were spent in Manhattan, while Doré lived in Michigan.

I got it.

Karen went on to show me other ways that I could improve my manuscript.

"I want to hear more about this," she said, "and less about that. You will probably want to flip this.... You might consider moving this up and shifting that down...."

I got it.

Stunned, I went back to Arizona feeling as if I were pulling arrows out of my chest—and convinced that my book was stillborn. Authors sometimes say that writing a book is not unlike giving birth to a baby. If you are told that your baby has serious birth defects, it is a painful blow to the heart. There may be surgeries that can repair the defects, but you must absorb the bad news before you can open your mind to those possibilities. And if you must be the surgeon, too, it takes more time before you can summon the courage to try to make your baby's life worth living.

A year later I was ready to seek a publisher. I'd learned that publishing is not an extension of writing. It's a business. And competition is HUGE. Nearly half a million books come out every year, and unless your name is Danielle Steele or J.K. Rowling, there is no point in approaching a commercial publisher.

Self-Publishing is not the same as the old "vanity presses" that charge a hefty fee and leave it to the author to store books in a basement or garage—and then sell them.

I started researching self-publishers and luckily heard about Mark Levine. After he wrote *The Fine Print of Self-Publishing*, in which he evaluated forty-five companies, he had learned so much that he formed his own company, Mill City Press. I eventually chose it as publisher for my book that I'd titled *Pagoda Dreamer*. They offer a variety of services, depending on whether you can do a lot for yourself (such as creating a website) or you want to pay them to do such things. Each element is separately priced, so you can create a package you can afford. The author makes 100 percent of the royalties.

Mill City Press, like the big commercial publishers, has several "imprints." One for children's books, one for science fiction, one for Christian readers, one for potential best sellers—and one for books with "literary merit" but a more limited audience. They accepted my book in the latter category: Langdon Street Press.

The give and take process of communicating my needs and wishes to the publisher's representative was complex. She sent each section of the manuscript as printed back to me by email for approval. Then I returned it electronically, pointing out errors and sometimes requesting changes. The labor went on for nine months (!), until I felt completely satisfied with the finished draft.

Following the birth of *Pagoda Dreamer* readers received my offspring with approval and affection.

馬

BOOK EIGHT
CANCER REDUX

*Death is not too high a price to pay
for having lived. Mountains never die,
nor do the seas or rocks or endless sky.
Through countless centuries of time, they stay
eternal, deathless. Yet they never live!
If choice were there, I would not hesitate
to choose mortality. Whatever Fate
demanded in return for life I'd give,
for never to have seen the fertile plains
nor heard the winds nor felt the warm sun on sands
beneath a salty sea, not touched the hands
of those I love—without these, all the gains
of timelessness would not be worth a day
of living and of loving; come what may.*

– "The Cost" by Dorothy Monroe

1

Party B4 Parting

In 2011 my husband Ethan had a kidney removed due to cancer. Meanwhile I fell in our kitchen and shattered my sacrum. The prescription for me was six weeks bedrest. When he came home from the hospital, we were crammed together in the small guest room. We looked at each other and simultaneously declared, "It's a Sign." It was time to move to Las Fuentes Retirement Resort.

On Ethan's mind was his desire to see me safely located in a senior community, in case his cancer recurred in another organ, rather than alone four miles outside of town. My desire was to see him free from concerns about home maintenance and property up-keep.

We moved October 11, 2011 into a spacious one-bedroom apartment with a small "L" off the living room which served as our home office. It suited us perfectly. We made new friends and enjoyed a lifestyle that included bus trips to plays in Mesa and picnics at distant lakes.

For three years, we hoped we had "dodged the bullet." But, in the spring of 2014, we learned that Ethan's cancer came back in the very area where his left kidney once lived. Retirement morphed into hospice routines as we devised how to spend our remaining time together.

When doctors gave Ethan about six months to live, my thoughts leaped ahead to the need to plan a memorial service. Others offered me alternative ideas.

Our interim UU minister suggested a church service *before* death. Our daughter Gretchen reminded us of the service she arranged for her biological father, at his Michigan congregation, before he died. He appreciated it so much— being able to hear tributes while alive.

I decided to adapt those ideas into a celebration of Ethan's life by throwing a party instead of a church service. Gretchen immediately pitched in ideas and planning tips as well as traveling from Alaska to be here for the occasion scheduled for June 7, 2014. We arranged to hold the event in the large Las Fuentes Social Room. Invitations posted around our retirement resort and Granite Peak congregation and emailed to other groups of friends promoted the "PARTY B4 PARTING."

Instead of a eulogy, we gave Ethan the opportunity to tell his own life story. He loved the idea and was energized by the task. Weakness seemed to leave him for several weeks. I asked individual friends to share selected readings and excerpted letters, and the "script" allowed time for people attending to voice memories and emotions.

The "party" aspect of the afternoon was contributed by Unitarian women headed by Nancy Snow who conceived delicious refreshments created by the team. Nancy Reid-McKee contributed an array of her own homemade desserts.

When the day arrived, we were astonished at the number of people who showed up. Ethan's son Bruce moved fireside couches out to the hallway to make room for more round tables and chairs. A Las Fuentes security guard estimated the crowd at two hundred and fifty people!

From Ethan's side at the head table, I could look out at faces of people who belonged to all the clubs and community organizations that Ethan had enjoyed. French speakers, stamp collectors, human rights activists, choral singers, art lovers, museum volunteers, OLLI members, religious liberals, and individual friends. Residents of our new home at Las Fuentes completed the heartwarming scene.

Following some opening readings, Phil Dixon led group singing and invited others to share memories or tributes. Our granddaughter Jordan Davis carried one of the portable microphones to people who wanted to speak. Connie Thacker read a poem she wrote and Andy Reti shared the following:

Goodbye to Ethan

"I have known Ethan for many years. At least 10, perhaps as many as 15.

A member of the Prescott French Club he brought charm and grace to our meetings. When he spoke in his quiet, elegant French we all listened, charmed by his fluent, clear language and the fascinating stories he would tell us about his life.

As Unitarians we have the luxury of being free to believe whatever we want to. We can be spiritual, agnostics or atheists. Many of us are refugees from more formal religions that did not satisfy our needs. But none of us, believers or unbelievers, know what's on the other side.

Ethan has made the brave decision to look the end in the eye and to make a statement: 'I'm in charge here!!' He may even be wagging a finger at fate as if to say, I am going to control how I am going to leave this world. Although Ethan has too much class and grace to wag a finger.

He has called us all together here to say goodbye to his family and friends. We have shared a lot in the past and now we are sharing his final voyage. And Ethan my friend, when you get there, send a postcard or an Email and let us know what's there

Have a good journey my friend. Go in peace."

Stan Brown read a passage from Ethan's mother's book titled "World On My Doorstep," in which she described raising her three "sturdy" sons in Europe.

Gretchen's daughter Leah, who was a great help with preparations, felt too sad to attend the party. I'm sorry she needed to skip it, but we understood her fear of embarrassing tears.

Lou Burrell's velvet voiced solo of "What a Wonderful World" made a perfect ending.

2

The Way It Went

"IT MIGHT BE TONIGHT," said the nurse gently, as she prepared to leave our apartment.

By "it," Kathy meant my husband Ethan's death.

He was asleep in a hospital bed that Good Samaritan Hospice had moved into our bedroom two days before. It made it easier for the nurse and aides to care for him, and the side bars relieved my worry that he would fall out of bed during the night.

I stretched out on the big brown leather recliner that Ethan loved. Loaned by a friend, it had offered him relaxing daytime comfort for many weeks. He would probably never sit there again. But, from its position at the foot of the hospital bed, I could watch his steady breathing.

From the day, five months earlier that our doctor, Ellen Bunch, hated to tell us that his cancer had returned, Ethan maintained that he felt "lucky." He was 87. Each of his two younger brothers died in their mid-fifties. As the oldest son, he never expected to outlive them. He had a cancerous kidney removed in 2011, and, for three years of no recurrence, we hoped that we had dodged the bullet.

When Ethan spoke of his "luck," that also referred to his lack of any pain. "They tell me I have a baseball-size tumor in my body, but you couldn't prove it by me," he liked to say, with a smile.

We'd been warned that the cancer might return in the right kidney or the bladder, but it came back in the space created by removal of the left kidney. That meant that a few sneaky malignant cells remained after surgery. Dear Dr. Michael Stanik wept with regret when he spoke with us about that.

"It's not your fault," Ethan assured him. "You surely believed you got them all."

"Yes," the doctor sighed. "But I'm just so sorry."

Recently, three years later, he told me he will never forget Ethan's character in that situation. "Such a fine man," he said.

...

Ethan was even grateful that his cancer was inoperable and untreatable.

"I have long believed that the quality of a life is far more important than its duration," he said. "And, from what I've heard, chemotherapy makes you sicker than your disease."

Given his age, he would have refused chemo or radiation if it had been suggested.

What Dr. Stanik did suggest was that we arrange for

hospice care sooner rather than later. "Many people believe that hospice is just a service to call at the very end," he said, "only when the patient needs morphine. They offer so much more."

We took that advice and deeply appreciated all the care that Good Samaritan provided. Ethan welcomed the "shower lady" who came to bathe him twice a week. I felt guilty that I couldn't help him that way, but we knew it would not be helpful if we both fell.

A final stroke of good luck, as we saw it, was that Ethan never had to enter the hospital. He was able to stay at home in our apartment, where we could meet the end together with no medical intervention, no drugs, no tubes, no wires. We could express whatever thoughts and feelings we wanted to share, without waiting for visiting hours.

The evening of August 4th, 2014, I sat up, alternately reading and watching my beloved sleep. As the hours passed, I felt increasingly cold. About three a.m. I decided to climb into my own bed, one of the twins that we centered on a king-size headboard. Ethan's half had been taken to the garage when the hospital bed was installed.

Ethan's breathing was shallow, but he seemed to be resting easy, so I succumbed to fatigue and stretched out in welcome warmth under my blanket.

Wakened by a ringing telephone, I heard the gentle voice of the hospice nurse asking, "So, how are you two today?" Surprised to see that the clock read 8:30, I stammered "We were still sleeping. Just a second, I'll check on Ethan."

As soon as I rolled over, I could see the change. Slipping out of bed on the side nearest him, I touched his pale grey skin. It was so cold, and he didn't seem to be breathing. With a sharp inhale of my own, I stumbled back to the telephone and managed to tell Kathy, "I'm pretty sure he's died."

"I'll be right over," she replied. Within five minutes she was in our bedroom. As soon as she confirmed Ethan's death, she called Dr. Sam Downing, her medical director, and offered to call Science Care, which was contracted to pick up "the body" for cremation.

Waiting with me, along with the nurse, was my dear friend Nancy Snow, who had been there the best part of several days. Her solid presence as she had tidied up the kitchen, bundled accumulated newspapers, heated her homemade soup and shared feelings, had been exactly the support I needed. Support she didn't receive when her husband died.

Now, she and Kathy left me alone with Ethan—to say our goodbye. Finally my tears flowed. Kathy had lowered the bed and its sidebars, so I could pull a chair close and rest my damp cheek on Ethan's hand.

On a teetertotter of emotions, I slid into rage at The Fates that took him from me, then felt lifted by gratitude for our thirty-five years together. I plummeted into self-pity over my future alone, then rose to tell him again how much I would miss him. I choked on the rise and fall of all those feelings before bumping bottom and accepting that I had to let him go. After kissing Ethan' face, I made way for the mortician's assistants.

Unwilling to watch as he was zipped into a body bag, I joined the other women in the living room. Resting my stinging eyes, I mused about the way Ethan's life had ended.

Often, the image of family members clustered around the foot of a bed, watching as their loved one breathes his last, is perceived as an ideal death. I briefly berated myself for not staying awake to hold Ethan's hand and murmur to him as he died. But soon, I smiled at another image. My husband, ever thoughtful and considerate, had gallantly waited until I was tucked into cozy rest before he slipped quietly away.

Once in a while, during the last few months, as his strength ebbed, Ethan would say something such as, "I'm sorry you have to do so much for me."

And I would remind him, "I not only want to help you, because you are my lover, but you deserve it," I said. "Remember how you took care of me after four joint replacements and two back surgeries?" He would smile and nod.

The day after the Party B4 Parting, Ethan asked me to sit beside him. Taking both my hands in his, he said, "I owe you an apology."

Surprised, I responded, "I can't imagine what for."

"I didn't give you enough support and appreciation for all the work that you and Gretchen were doing for the party. I just didn't really understand what would happen." Reaching up to touch my face, he said, "It was just wonderful, and I want to thank you from the bottom of my heart."

A newspaper feature about Ethan's party, published in Prescott's Daily Courier, inspired a number of people to follow his example. If they didn't host a large party, they at least held a small dinner with some of Granddad's close friends. It is, of course, not possible if a person dies in a head-on collision or of a sudden heart attack. But, if a family has time, I recommend it.

A few times, during his final illness, I teased Ethan about leaving me behind. "It's not fair." I whined. "You get all the tributes and loving attention and I have to stay on alone and cope with everything by myself."

We chuckled. He knew I was kidding. He was also sure that I knew he didn't want to leave me. He did all he could to smooth the solo path I would have to follow. Shortly after the diagnosis, he began to train me to become a widow. He went through his desk drawers and file cabinet, discarding outdated correspondence, unimportant forms and useless notes. He left me a three-page typed memo listing all the people and places I would need to notify after his death.

He also researched the best place for me to sell his stamp collection, and left instructions on how to contact the Swiss Auction House. The saga of following those instructions deserves its own chapter.

Deep gratitude fills me again as I think of how lucky we were. Most people have relatives or friends who divorced a first spouse but never found "Mr. or Mrs. Right" going forward. Ethan and I were not only right for each other when we entered a second marriage, we grew closer with every year. We were kindred souls who enriched each other's lives beyond measure.

I dreaded life without him, and it surely is a lonely one. But I know that the only way to avoid the pain of parting is never to love.

3

Selling His Stamps

ETHAN was a stamp collector. As he faced his death, he wrote me a letter containing detailed instructions on how to package and ship his extensive collection to be sold at auction in Switzerland.

It was in Switzerland where, as a young boy, he was introduced to the hobby. His father's secretary at the Carnegie Endowment saved her "foreign" stamps for him and showed him how to paste them into albums according to country. Ethan lived in her country from ages four to eight, when his father's work took the family there.

After years of keeping and mounting stamps from "the world," as he put it, he had most recently narrowed the field to Switzerland. Therefore, he turned to a Swiss auction house when he was ready to have his heirs dispose of his collection.

This is part of the letter he wrote me in July 2014:

Your auction contact in Switzerland is Christina Bamford-Rolli. Her Email address will come up when you enter her name.

Their address is:

Rolli Schar AG
Seidenhofstrasse 2
CH 6003 Luzern

When it is time to ship the collections, have Federal Express come in to package and ship the collection by *Registered* mail. You will not need to insure the shipment because it is already insured for $75,000 through the American Philatelic Society. Rolli-Schar will take on the insurance obligation once they receive the collections. There are five albums on the top shelf next to the computer; 13 albums on the second shelf; 10 hingeless smaller albums on the third shelf; and 8 special stamp catalogs on the fourth shelf. THEY ALL GO.

As soon as I attempted to carry out Ethan's wishes, I learned that Federal Express does not provide such in-home service. I was faced with the challenge of finding a friend who would load up the albums and take them—safely—to FedEx.

When Ethan's son Bruce heard my dilemma, he offered to take all the albums to his workplace, where he had access to the needed materials for packaging. I agreed, and he did a meticulous job of protecting them for shipping.

Ethan had also instructed me to:

Email Ms. Bamford-Rolli when collections have been taken for shipping giving her the Fedex package number and estimated delivery date; and ask her to confirm receipt. Give her your mailing address so that she can send the auction proceeds payable to you; and specify payment should be in US Dollars.

Weeks stretched out as Bruce tried to discover a cheaper way of getting the stamp albums overseas. FedEx was going to charge about $700 per box for four boxes. I researched some other options, but then the Swiss auction house offered to arrange everything through DHL for about $500 per package. This still seemed outrageous to Bruce, so he did not give them the address for pick up, and time kept slipping away.

Meanwhile, thru my email correspondence with Christina, I learned that we had to get everything to Switzerland by Nov. 20th, because they had to prepare the lots by November 30—for the next auction, which I assumed was December. If we missed that auction, they said, it would be *more than a year* before they could be sold in February *2016*. Bruce wanted to know why, but that didn't matter. After discussing it further, I sent him an email in 36 pt. font saying, "SOONEST NOT CHEAPEST."

When I explained the delay to Christina, she told me, "I am so sorry you've been worried. Our offer meant the shipping would go on *our* DHL account and you would not have to front any money now. The costs will come out of the auction proceeds before you receive your portion of the sales."

So, Bruce finally sent them the necessary information. Whew!! I told him that I deeply appreciated his desire to save me money, and that I was also very grateful that, in the end, he saw the need to act. I just couldn't bear the thought of letting Ethan down on this task....

Bill Hess, a New Jersey stamp dealer, later told me that the Nov. 30 deadline for preparing the lots was probably not for a December auction but to get the information to a *printer* who is going to create the *catalog* for a February 2015 auction. If so, then the February 2016 date for the next auction (of Swiss stamps) made more sense.

Ethan also wrote:

> It is my deep desire that the proceeds from their sale go to
> the Endowment Fund at Granite Peak Unitarian Universalist
> Congregation to help fund attendance at UUA General
> Assemblies or Leadership Training offered by the Pacific
> Southwest District...

Earlier I had asked him, "Why don't you sell the collection
yourself and have the joy of making a large gift to the church?"

Jack Wood, accountant, explained, "Ethan would have
to pay tax on the auction proceeds. And he can't give the
collection itself to the congregation because it is not the
type of gift a church can accept. If you wanted to present an
organ, fine. But not a stamp collection."

"Therefore," he said, "The best move is to leave the stamps
to Judy, who will not be taxed. She can sell the collection
and carry out your wishes."

So Ethan instructed me to:

> Deposit the auction proceeds in your checking account; and
> then write a check to GPUUC for the same amount with
> "Endowment Fund" on the memo line.

The Swiss auction went off as scheduled, attracting
wealthy buyers. I received our proceeds and the catalog is
now among my keepsakes. The Granite Peak Endowment
Committee soon set up a fund in Ethan's name.

The Sunday morning service when I presented a check
to Granite Peak was a thrilling occasion for me. It was the
first time that most members learned of the bequest, and
we received a standing ovation.

During the five years since, every time someone is named as an annual recipient of the Ethan Davis Scholarship, it warms my heart. I feel proud of Ethan for conceiving the idea of the gift. And I am grateful that the delays in the process of packaging and shipping did not derail his dream.

4

Military Honors

I CONSIDER MYSELF to be a patriotic pacifist. To some, that might sound like a contradiction. But I maintain that I can be a proud American while loathing war. I believe that world leaders generally fail to strive toward peaceful solutions to international disputes. They leap all too quickly to engage armies in mutual slaughter. As Bob Dylan asked, "How many deaths will it take 'til they know that too many people have died?"

But I also accept that military action may be necessary when nations are called upon to combat evil tyrants, such as Adolph Hitler. In late 1941, when Hitler's ally, Imperial Japan, attacked the United States Naval base in Hawaii, our country entered what came to be known as World War II. To raise an army, all able-bodied young men were being drafted into military service as soon as they turned eighteen.

My husband, Ethan Davis, finished his sophomore year at Columbia College shortly after his eighteenth birthday in

February 1945. To avoid being called into the Infantry, he enlisted in the U.S. Navy. After basic training, he expected to be sent into active duty. Instead, to his surprise, he was spot-commissioned an Ensign and assigned to an officer program to learn to speak, read and write Japanese!

The Navy, by then, had learned that it was easier to teach a new language to people who were already proficient in other languages. Having grown up in Europe, Ethan spoke fluent French and had studied Russian. He and others like him were being trained to be interpreters in a planned Allied invasion of Japan, which was expected to be launched in 1946. The language program was conducted on the campus of Oklahoma A&M University in Stillwater. The teachers were American citizens of Japanese origin. They were all volunteers who had come from the internment camps. Ethan often said, "It amazed me that despite their families' incarceration they wanted to help the American war effort."

The Japanese Language School was the top priority program in the US Navy at the time. "Once you were ordered to report," Ethan recalled, "only the Secretary of the Navy could have you reassigned. If you failed a test, you were just dropped back to what you had last passed. We were warned that if we could not average 95% on exams in the first three months that we would flunk out before six months, because we would never catch up! That year-long training was the most difficult and challenging learning experience of my life, and I am not sure I could have done it without the pressure of the war."

Luckily, Ethan never had to serve in an invasion of Japan. America's use of atomic bombs ended World War II. After 18 months in uniform, he was discharged and went home to New York City to complete his college education at Columbia. He remained in the Naval Reserve until 1950.

Ethan was proud to have served his country in an unusual way, but he also understood my aversion to military combat. My lifelong antipathy, fostered by pacifist parents, was reinforced for me during the Vietnam War. In common with many Americans in that era, I considered it an illegal, immoral action in which thousands of precious lives were sacrificed for a needless cause.

In 2009, Ethan was impressed by a ceremony in which a deceased friend's ashes were placed in a niche in a wall at the Prescott National Cemetery. It is a privilege available to any honorably discharged veteran. When he told me that he wanted me to arrange that honor for him after he died, Ethan knew that I was disturbed by the whole idea. I dreaded the day I would have to listen to a twenty-one-gun salute. He never explained why the rituals appealed to him. He just asked me to see that his wishes were carried out. Knowing what it meant to him, I never dreamed of refusing.

I also never dreamed how meaningful the ceremony would be for me.

After cancer took Ethan's life in August 2014, I made the necessary calls to the Veterans Administration and the local American Legion Post. Ethan's son Bruce chose the date, Thursday, September 25, because Jordan, his fourteen-year-old daughter, had that day off from school. It turned out to be ideal. Puffy white clouds floated in an Arizona-blue sky, nudged by just enough breeze for perfect comfort. I was pleased to see that The Prescott National Cemetery is splendidly maintained, with flat, ground-level gravestones set in a vast, manicured lawn, where policy forbids cheap decorations.

Our granddaughter Jordan and her father Bruce spent the night before at my apartment and drove me to our designated spot on the sloping, grassy hill, where Dan Tillmans and four other uniformed members of the American Legion Honor Guard awaited us. We were soon joined by Bruce's wife Lisa and eighteen friends who took seats on backed benches under a shade tree facing the "Columbarium Wall." Looking above and beyond it to the west, we could see Prescott's landmark "Thumb Butte" in the distance. As I relaxed in relief at seeing arrangements unfolding as we hoped, a sense of serenity stilled me for what followed.

The brief military service opened with a bugler playing "Taps." That powerful musical symbol of farewell set the tone and the mood. The loud rifle volleys fired behind us were startling but seemed appropriate. Not twenty-one guns, but three men each shooting seven times. Later, the cemetery director ceremoniously presented the spent shells to Bruce.

The ritual unfolding, saluting and refolding of a large American flag affected me deeply. The uniformed naval officers, one man, one woman, were so earnest and respectful about their task that it was surprisingly moving. Then, when the gracious young man approached me to present the neat, compact triangle, he said, "From the President of the United States, the United States Navy and a grateful nation, we offer you this flag in tribute for your loved one's service." That's when my tears spilled out. Later, I repeated his words to Jordan when I gave her the folded flag to keep. She was moved, too. Bruce bought her a triangular case for the precious keepsake of her beloved "Grampy."

The military honors ended with a colorfully kilted bag piper, Don Mansfield, playing "Amazing Grace." Simply beautiful! The music softly faded as he walked ceremoniously down and away.

Then two friends—the Rev. Sue Nauman and Peter Eldridge—conducted a simple, optional personal portion of the service. The reading of two special poems bookended the brief description of Ethan's unusual time in the Navy that I've recounted above.

The cemetery director then invited Bruce forward to accompany him to Wall "D" and place Ethan's ashes in a niche on the top row. A park employee tightened the four screws of a temporary cover. The following week, an engraved marble cover with mandatory information and our personal inscription was added. I was pleased to learn that the available symbols include the "flaming chalice" of Unitarian Universalism. Below that, it reads:

DAVIS
ETHAN I.
LTJG USN WWII
1927 – 2014
QUIET DIGNITY
ETHICAL SOUL
AU REVOIR

Initially, after Bruce and I devised phrases that described his dad and fit the letter limit, he didn't understand why I wanted the final line. I reminded him of how proud Ethan always felt about his fluency with the French language, and how, whenever we traveled among French-speaking people, they would marvel at his perfect accent and maintain that they could not believe he was American, not Parisian. Bruce acknowledged that reason.

The rituals associated with military honors were far lovelier and more meaningful than I expected. Although Ethan never tried to persuade me, while he lived, he probably expected that they would be.

I kept wishing I could tell him, "NOW I get why you wanted us to experience this ceremony!"

I like to imagine that he knew.

Later, a Michigan friend asked whether the ceremony gave me a sense of closure, or at least completion.

Yes.

Ethan is not in a niche in a wall. But I feel completion for having carried out his wishes, for having understood his reasons, and for having had this profoundly moving way of bidding a final farewell to his earthly presence.

Ethan will live on in the hearts of all who knew him—as I will someday dwell in the memories of my beloved family and cherished friends.

That, I believe, is immortality.

馬

BOOK NINE

His Legacy

"The past is never dead. It's not even past. All of us labor in webs spun long before we were born—webs of heredity and environment, of desire and consequence, of history and eternity. Haunted by wrong turns and roads not taken, we pursue images perceived as new, but whose provenance dates to the dim dramas of childhood, which are themselves but ripples of consequence echoing down the generations. The quotidian demands of life distract from this resonance of events, but some of us feel it always."

– William Faulkner

1

The Archives

IN 1995, when Ethan and I decided to spend our retirement years in Arizona instead of New Jersey, we faced downsizing all our belongings, including family memorabilia. It was then that I remembered what Katy Ryor suggested when we met in China. When she learned that my father was Benjamin March, she suggested that the Freer-Sackler Archives at the Smithsonian would be glad to have materials from his professional career.

I contacted Jan Stewart, the Asian Art curator in Washington, DC. In addition to giving her a brief description of my father's career, I explained that he had once held a Freer Fellowship to conduct some of his research. My hopes were not high, but I was curious.

The response was almost as overwhelming to me as Katy's original reaction to seeing my father's name. Dr. Stewart and other Freer-Sackler art historians wrote me of their delight in my offer to donate the "Benjamin March Papers" to their archives. Arrangements were made and a date set for us to deliver the boxes.

First, I went through Daddy Ben's journals and photocopied many pages of his observations. Certain passages were simply beautiful or fascinating. Others had a personal meaning to me—such as his descriptions of meeting my mother and a few notations about their courtship and marriage. I also kept some of the photographs—of their wedding, family members and close friends—as well as the pictures of their homes.

...

On a warm spring day, a Washington-area friend, who had been with us on our tour of China and heard my story, drove us as close as possible to the entrance of the museum. He double-parked while Ethan and I carried in four hefty cartons of memorabilia.

Inside, Colleen Hennessey, a soft-spoken young archivist, greeted us warmly, guided us to the archives and invited us to spread out the materials. As we looked over the journals and photos and lecture notes, she kept reiterating how grateful the museum was to receive this magnificent gift! It amused us to note that she wore white gloves in handling all these fragile books—books that had been packed and stacked haphazardly in a succession of my basements and garages for so many years.

During his time in Beijing, my father had met older Americans who lived in China. He had been granted interviews with some of these revered scholars and had been given permission to photograph the interiors of their homes.

Soon after our donation, a Freer-Sackler historian found Ben March's observations and pictures of great value to him. He was writing a book about a former Freer staff member, Carl Whiting Bishop, who worked in China between 1923 and 1934. Ben's materials gave the writer information he didn't know existed, fleshing out his own research.

Learning that scholars such as this would go on putting my father's papers to similar good use was deeply gratifying. Perhaps, had I turned them over to the institution years earlier, other uses could have been made of them. But it had simply never occurred to me that they would mean so much to people in his field.

How lucky it was that Ethan and I chose a Smithsonian Tour of China—a tour that employed a young art historian who revered my father's work, increased my understanding and appreciation for his career, and steered me in the direction of sharing the materials I had with people who valued them.

If my grown children or their children are ever curious about their maternal grandfather or great grandfather, they can visit the archives. Donning white gloves, they can discover, as his daughter did, that Ben March was a remarkable young man who ventured to a far-off land, absorbed its culture, and set scholarly standards that still matter to those who lived after him.

2

Legacy

AFTER I MAILED the first copies of *Pagoda Dreamer* to family members and close friends, my mind turned to other people who might be interested in knowing that this book had been published.

Remembering the young woman who had been so helpful to us when I donated my father's "collected papers" to the Freer/Sackler Archives at the Smithsonian, I sent an email to the "info" address, asking whether Colleen Hennessey was still employed there and if anyone could tell me how to get in touch with her. My message went out on December 8, 2009.

A few days later, I received a phone call from David Hogge, who identified himself as the current "head archivist" and said that he had been trying unsuccessfully for months to get in touch with me! Curiously, his internet search for Judith March Davis ended in Mesa (near Phoenix), about 100 miles from where I live. Not me.

He made no attempt to disguise the excitement in his voice as he described the reason for his quest and delight in "Contact!" For the entire month of November, more than 60 of Benjamin March's photographs and his travel diaries were exhibited at an art museum in Hangzhou, China."

In response to my astonishment, David explained that Hangzhou's leading citizens were hoping to have their city designated as a United Nations World Heritage Site—or at the very least "The Honeymoon Capitol" of Asia. When they learned that my parents had honeymooned there in 1925, they believed that publicity about this choice by a newlywed American couple could help promote the cause.

When the officials learned that Mr. March's collected papers were housed in the Freer/Sackler Archives, they formally requested that the pictures and diaries related to Hangzhou be loaned for a special exhibition. David Hogge had been intimately connected to the arrangements and had flown to China for the show's opening. Had he been able to locate the honeymooners' daughter, I would have been invited to attend as well.

Colleen Hennessey had retired.

During our first phone conversation, David said, "I know that Benjamin died young. But tell me, whatever happened to Dorothy after his death?" Chuckling to myself, I told him that I had just written and published a whole book on that subject!

When he pressed me for a brief account then and there, I replied, "Well, she had a young child to support, so she went to work for the University of Michigan in the Department of the History of Art and was eventually Supervisor of Photographs and Slides...." Whereupon, David was the one chuckling. He had held the exact same job in that department long after her retirement, when he earned a graduate degree in art history!

During the following year or two, David and I exchanged frequent emails, about our own lives as well as Benjamin March. David's wife is Japanese. They met and married in Japan, where David was studying. Their one son studied at MIT. I mailed the archivist a copy of my memoir chapter titled "He Set the Standards," so that he would have the back story behind my donation of my father's papers.

In email attachments, David sent me newspaper clippings (mostly published in Chinese) about the Hangzhou exhibition. It was a very professional show—with Ben's photos enlarged, matted and attractively framed. Elderly people, David said, were thrilled to see pictures of places and artifacts that had vanished years ago. "They would put their noses very near the glass to see small creeks spanned by decorative wooden bridges, rickshaws and sedan chairs, and long-gone little shops," he said.

Outside the museum a 10 x 20 ft. blowup of a photograph of my parents was used as an advertising poster. The couple was posed in matching cotton robes at the girls' school where they rented rooms. Doré is sitting on Ben's lap as they gaze into each other's eyes. If I had remembered that such a heartwarming picture was among the scenic views of Hangzhou that I donated to the archives, I would certainly have used it in my book.

I wondered what happened to the work of other photographers during the 1920's and asked David whether they were lost during the Cultural Revolution. Indeed so,

---

he replied. "Today the Chinese are lamenting the loss, and people feel it is safe to bring out their old family albums," he wrote. "There are many good photographs in tourist collections, but March really got off the beaten path and photographed things otherwise unrecorded."

When I asked David why Ben's diaries were included, he wrote, "The writing is about the best travel writing I have ever read; expository, deeply personal and imbued with deep optimism of a young man in love and with a whole life ahead of him. His words and his photos stand on their own."

After I sent David a copy of *Pagoda Dreamer*, he said, "You descend from a family of writers, and it shows. I couldn't put it down." He agreed to make suggestions for anything I should ask my publisher to change in the second printing and offered a small correction to my description of the Boxer Rebellion. Empathizing with my regret over errors in my research sources, he said that, even in China, it is difficult to find accurate information. He said he felt "honored" to write the review that appears on the website: *www.pagodadreamer.com*

Motivated to look through more of the materials I had donated, David occasionally sent me electronic images, asking if I could identify the people in the photographs. I enjoyed giving him names when I knew them.

In the spring of 2012, David visited us. The tall, thin, soft-spoken man, then 51, spent two nights and one full day in Prescott, examining the rest of what he calls "The Benjamin March Collection."

Most of what I still had was family memorabilia which, as I predicted, David Hogge did not want. He is only interested in my father's career, not his Boy Scout scrapbook or WWI photo album. But he was delighted with certain finds and selected a stack of photos and publications that he believes will be of great interest to various researchers. He also told me that my father's name *still* comes up at scholarly conferences, such as one in New York City in February of that year.

He listed (on his laptop) and photographed everything he wanted to add to the existing Benjamin March materials in the archives. Those he later showed to his boss to get permission. Then we were instructed to take everything to Federal Express which properly boxed things up (as if they were rare artifacts) to be shipped to Washington. David said that it would have been absolutely forbidden for him to stuff things in his carry-on.

We own a large (40x26") framed portrait of my father by Michigan artist Paul Honoré in the style of a Chinese ancestor portrait. David Hogge wrote, "…I would like to push for acquisition here. It would add to our growing collection of other distinguished scholars." We later learned it would not be hung on the wall of a gallery. The Smithsonian has, in its archives, a collection of *scroll* paintings of Americans by Chinese artists. So, even if David received permission to accept a framed oil painting, it would not be displayed!

As it turned out, I was happy to keep the painting. Our review of memorabilia that day David spent in our apartment made me quite nostalgic about my father. Behind the "distinguished scholar" lies my "Daddy Ben." My husband Ethan agreed with this decision, as he loved the painting, too, and we didn't want it just stuck away in the dark. If someone wants to borrow the portrait for display, the Archives will contact me.

A Chinese scholar who mounted a 2014 exhibition about the actor Mei Lanfang, borrowed copies of Ben's slim volume of photographs of his hands. Titled "Orchid Hands of Mei Lanfang." She said it enhanced the show about the famous female interpreter.

Another Chinese scholar, based in Boston, asked my permission to translate my father's diary about his and Doré's honeymoon in Hangzhou. Ben's early China diaries were among the papers I donated in 1995. His descriptions of Hangzhou had already been translated into Chinese to be available with the catalog of another exhibition of his photographs at the art museum there. In 2016, Sarah Shay (Xie Xiaopei) supervised publication of "March's Honeymoon Diary" which includes Ben's original pages (with typing errors) "for the cultural significance," she said, "of his beautifully written observations." She arranged with the Hangzhou museum to send me ten copies which are treasured by family members and others.

When I told David Hogge that I longed for color photos, he replied, "I rather like Benjamin's simple black and white images, so eloquent in their brevity. And perfect with his lovely descriptions of happily exploring the old city with Dorothy."

David also shipped us a stack of current Chinese art journals, many of which contained articles by or about Ben! It blows my mind that essays/lectures written by a young American so long ago can still have meaning to Chinese scholars today.

David Hogge resigned his post at the Freer/Sackler Archives in spring 2018. He had no other immediate professional plans. He expected to return to the northwest, where he grew up. "Anywhere but Washington DC in today's political climate," he sighed. "One of my great regrets is that we have not been able to finish up the Benjamin March diaries project, but I am hopeful that the museum will remain committed to supporting the Archives."

All the interest in the work of Benjamin March, nearly eighty-five years after his death, is truly astonishing to me. Meeting the young art historian Katy Ryor on our tour of China opened my eyes. Her suggestion that I donate my father's papers to the Smithsonian reopened widespread scholarly interest in his work. My decision to write a book about my mother led to further interest in my father! If I hadn't written *Pagoda Dreamer* and believed that Colleen Hennessey would enjoy reading it, I would never have known the long-ranging impact of his brief life.

Today, reflecting on my own *long* life, I regret the emotional energy I wasted in early years by turning my back on my heritage. My mother's accounts of my father's career followed the clichéd path of in one ear and out the other. Now, how much I wish she could know the pride I feel in the continued acclaim for my "Daddy Ben."

Made in the USA
San Bernardino, CA
23 January 2020

63285265R00212